UNASSISTED LIVING

UNASSISTED LIVING
AGELESS HOMES FOR LATER LIFE

Wid Chapman and Jeff Rosenfeld

THE MONACELLI PRESS

Library of Congress Control Number: 2011933746
ISBN: 978-1-58093-302-5

Printed in China

10 9 8 7 6 5 4 3 2 1

Designed by Think Studio, NYC

www.monacellipress.com

ACKNOWLEDGMENTS

Our book is called *Unassisted Living*, but we could never have written it without assistance, encouragement, and support from many quarters.

First and foremost, we want to thank our editor, Elizabeth White, for her vision, her patience, and her insights. Our book was shaped by her, and with her, from start to finish. Many thanks, too, to John Clifford of Think Studio, who has created this handsome and compelling design.

We are also indebted to the architects, designers, and boomers who shared their stories, and in many cases invited us to their studios, their homes, and their communities. Without exception, everyone we approached for interviews was generous both with time and with information. Typically, when we mentioned the premise, and especially the title of the book, the response was "Wow! You're really on to something."

Most of the boomers that we interviewed and visited in the process of researching this book would recommend friends and relatives—also boomers on the verge of retirement—who had created their own versions of "Unassisted Living." If we had more time, space, and energy, we could have included many more of the homes where boomers are preparing to live when (and if) they retire.

Special thanks to James B. Weil for permitting us to visit and include the barn which he transported from Vermont to Connecticut, and then added on to his home. The saga of that barn parallels the saga of many boomers as they approach later life, and we included it for that very reason. Like so many boomers, James Weil has been energized by retirement. Only in later life did he have the time, energy and support system to locate, transport, and attach a colonial barn to his home. In this accomplishment, we see the essence of how boomers are rethinking "home" in later life. It becomes the place where they can reinvent themselves. Like Weil and his home, the lives (and later-life homes) of many boomers will be recognizable—but they will also have changed.

Thanks also to Tim Duggan and his dedicated staff at MakeIt Right NOLA. This project, with generous funding from the Brad Pitt Foundation, has begun to create a new, sustainable, and flood-resistant community in New Orleans's 9th Ward in the wake of Hurricane Katrina. Many of those displaced by the floodwaters were boomers and their families, and from Mr. Duggan, his staff, and the residents of New Orleans we discovered another dimension of unassisted living. We have called it the Quest For Community. Many of these boomers, faced with the destruction of their homes and their city, decided to stay in New Orleans and rebuild their homes and their communities in later life. We have been inspired by what we have learned from a small but significant group of boomers in post-Katrina New Orleans; and we acknowledge how successful they have been in creating sustainable homes, and communities for themselves.

Our book has been built upon conversations with architects, and boomers, but also upon the encouragement of our families and friends.

Wid Chapman would like to thank dedicated staff members at Wid Chapman Architects who helped research the book: Carmen Santaella, Aaron Lee, Stephanie Schenk, Jesse Mueller and Michelle Kim. Wid dedicates this book to his parents, Allan and Amy, and his children, Kiran, Anejli, and Skyler.

Jeff Rosenfeld would like to thank Joan Bloomgarten, a friend and colleague at Hofstra University, for input at the time that the contents of this book were taking shape. But most of all, he thanks his wife, Sue, who is an inspirational editor, critic, and soulmate and Jordan and his family. Jeff dedicates this book "To the guys: Jordan, Ethan, and William."

We believe that the time has come to acknowledge the new frontiers of home- and community-design that boomers are exploring, and we also take full responsibility for everything presented in the following pages. That said, we proudly present *Unassisted Living*.

DESIGNED FOR VITALITY: AT HOME IN LATER LIFE

Cali Williams Yost calls himself a Workplace Flexibility Coach. Boomers, now in their fifties and early sixties, often pay him handsomely to plan a "delayed retirement" for them. Yost helps his clients, part of the generation of 51 million men and women born between 1946 and 1964, to create a mix of work, leisure, and social activism. Yost tells them, "You have to understand that this is not going to be your parents' retirement." He could add that many boomers have created homes for themselves that are as eclectic and creative as their delayed retirements. Now, more than ever before, boomers are building and designing space to house a new mix of work, play, and social relationships.

Boomers want a lot from the homes where they will typically live for a decade or more after they retire. Of course they want the space to be safe and comfortable, but in the process of researching this book, we learned they expect more than just safety and comfort. We conducted informal interviews with twenty-five homeowners, all in their early sixties, many of whom were on the verge of retirement. Time and again, they told us they also expect their homes to be activity centers, where they can continue to be involved with consulting, hobbies, even meditation and yoga. No generation has ever placed such contradictory demands on later-life housing. The demand for both ease and engagement is new, a factor that will become increasingly important in home design as more boomers retire. *Unassisted Living* celebrates new directions in home design that respond to these sometimes competing demands.

The most interesting news is that many hippies-turned-boomers continue to flaunt authority, even in their early sixties. Our sample of homeowners and homebuyers confirms that they are planning to install grab bars in bathrooms and to retrofit kitchens to make them safer and more compact—sensible decisions for those growing older. But many in the same group also expect to be aging in houses with steep, switchback stairways. Many of the homes included in this book have universally designed kitchens and baths and are as green and sustainable as they can be. Yet they defy conventional wisdom by being too large or too open; too dark or too bright. In fact, they are a lot like boomers themselves, and they reflect the unique stamp that boomers will bring to the homes and apartments where they will be living when they retire.

As environmentalist Rick Andreen recently noted, "Boomers want it green." He underscores the fact that boomers often have deep knowledge of and personal interest in environmental issues, making this the first generation of older adults with significant environmental awareness. The attraction to green/sustainable homes is already manifesting in two types of unassisted living. The first is the retrofitting of existing homes to include more solar power, water conservation, and fossil-fuel controls. The second is the development of cohousing communities that are green/sustainable by intent. .Make It Right NOLA, currently under construction in New Orleans, boasts that it will someday be the largest, greenest neighborhood of single-family homes in America. Many boomers are not only incorporating green and sustainable features into homes and apartments; they are making these into lifestyle choices. A recent survey by Harris Interactive finds that four out of five boomers are concerned about the environmental legacy they will leave behind for their grandchildren's generation.

Unassisted Living presents an alternate universe in which people live independently or in supportive communities of their own making. We are aware, of course, that many people will become frail and will have to deal with chronic illness, both physical and cognitive. But we already see alternatives to long-term care and assisted living. The homes featured this book are places where people will be living on their own, usually with people they love and enjoy, with the expectation of longer, healthier lives. We have selected thirty-three homes, including single-family dwellings, townhouses, apartments, and getaway cottages, that vary widely in terms of location, age, style, size, and expense. What they have in common, however, is the fact that they have been designed with vitality in mind. These are places where people can age gracefully and continue to blossom in later life.

The challenge for boomers is to remain engaged and live life to the fullest. Many are well aware that their own parents had moved into senior housing at about the same age that they are right now. The problem, as most boomers see it, is that senior housing offers a less active lifestyle than they want or need. Traditional senior housing, especially long-term care facilities, is isolated from the surrounding community, and boomers find that unacceptable. Instead, boomers are strategically planning homes and communities where they can continue to be engaged with their families, their hobbies, their consulting, and their friends. A generation fixated on health, fitness, and social connection is now planning to multi-task in later life. For example, many will telecommuting from the dining room, deck, or potting shed well into their sixties or seventies. One boomer explains it this way:

> Most of us feel that retirement is a thing of the past and have continued to improve our communities so we can remain actively engaged in them for years to come. Our biggest challenge so far has been convincing policymakers to think differently about how and where we Boomers want to grow old.

Boomers are insisting on living in homes and communities where they can remain connected to friends, family, and work. And yet, they *are* growing older. Active as they are, most boomers still need smaller, more compact homes, with fewer steps to climb, less lawn to mow, lots of counter space and waist-high kitchen shelving, and easier access to bath or shower. It's asking a lot of any home or community to provide all of this. Strategic design anticipates the needs of aging minds and bodies without cutting back on style or sustainability.

All of the houses and apartments in this book were created for people who are retired or anticipating retirement and built between 2000 and 2010. About half were commissioned by those who live in them; the balance were designed by architects who envisioned spaces that would encourage aging in place. We have organized them thematically, according to the basic strategy that underlies their design: downsizing in an urban setting; multigenerational living; communities based on shared interests; home-centered work and healthcare; rural life; adaptation on of a second home; adaptation of a primary residence; and affordable solutions. None of these categories is absolute and various houses fit into more than one. Nevertheless, the basic strategies are clear and relevant as the first boomers reach age sixty-five.

Bistro Living: Downsized for Vitality

A significant number of boomers will reject suburbia, even if they have lived in single-family suburban homes for years or even decades. Many crave something more glamorous and more urbane, what Jan Mitchell calls "bistro living." It is familiar that many Boomers want to be absolved from maintaining the yard, the pool, and a sprawling suburban home. Once they have sold those houses, a growing number of boomers are moving to apartments, townhouses, or studios in urban areas. This interest in sophisticated living has kept surprisingly large numbers of boomers from relocating to planned communities.

Three Generations Together: Multi-Family Homes and Communities

Boomers are entering later life with the most diverse set of family and kinship ties of any generation in American history. Instead of living in an empty nest, many are already managing "refilled nests." This is the first generation to be entering later life with such a high incidence of remarriages, step-families, and step-grandchildren. More boomers have at least one living parent, who is elderly and may need full-time care. Some refilled nests will be two-generational. A small but growing number will be three-generational, including boomers, their offspring, and either an aging parent, or a passel of grandchildren. In some cases the family lives together in a home or compound and in others there are separate guest quarters for grandparents or relatives who visit frequently enough to be considered "regulars." Most boomers want at least one room where relatives can live or stay when they visit.

Getaways

We know a retired couple who own a spacious apartment in Chevy Chase, Maryland, and a gracious beach house on the Delaware shore. Five years ago, they downsized from a stately house to the apartment. The apartment is their primary residence for the time being, but they are preparing for the day when they will move permanently to the beach house. They have already installed a small elevator. They built two suites on the second level: the master suite with bath, and a guest suite with its own bath. This level will someday become the primary living space, and the rest of the house will be more or less closed up.

"If we are lucky," they say, "the guest room will still be for visitors and guests." But given their health, they might someday need to hire a home health aide, who would sleep in that guest suite.

The homes featured in this section are of two varieties. There is a typical getaway home in a seaside resort. And then there is a guest cottage, which stands just a few hundred yards away from a larger and much older home. The guest cottage was built for the occasional weekend visitor, but it is so cozy that the aging owners will eventually make it their primary residence.

Getaway homes are an unappreciated component of senior housing. A number of boomers are planning to relocate to their getaways or will spend increasing amounts of time there as they get older. For both of these reasons, it is worth highlighting getaways that are fun places requiring less maintenance and up-keep than primary residences.

Off The Grid: Later Life in Wide-Open Spaces

We know an elderly woman in Manhattan who could afford to live anywhere she wants but insists upon staying in her somewhat shabby apartment. When asked why, she said, "I wouldn't want to live more than twenty minutes from my doctors!" Like so many urbanites in their late seventies or early eighties, she is now almost trapped in a neighborhood she once loved. A combination of physical frailty, ethnic succession, and urban decline now make it impossible for her to leave. But hers may be the last generation to be constrained in this way. Advances in technology, communications, and transportation are changing the options in later life. For perhaps the first time, people on the verge of retirement can live anywhere they want and still feel that they are always connected to health-providers, stock brokers, and, of course, to family and friends.

The houses in this chapter explore the freedom to live in remote areas well into one's seventies or eighties. We examine single-family homes designed for retirement, or semi-retirement, in isolated and/or wide-open spaces: a desert in Texas, a canyon in Wyoming, and on a steep Iowa hillside. It used to be that if and when older people ventured into these locations, they bought homes in communities that had been developed in the Arizona desert or near the Florida Everglades. But those homes, although far away, were nestled in manicured communities. Our focus is on single-family homes, which distinguishes them from the senior housing of yesteryear.

Working and Healing From Home

Many homes designed for people in later life automatically include a home office or studio to provide a space where residents can continue working and pursue hobbies at home. This generation has no intention of disengaging from work or physical activity at age sixty-five. A sample of boomers who were surveyed on this subject say they do not want to retire. They prefer to live and work in age-integrated neighborhoods, or communities. In other words, many boomers plan to grow older in the towns or neighborhoods where they are already living.

At this age, most boomers are still in good health and have not yet contemplated the impact of chronic or catastrophic illness could have on their careers and their living arrangements. But advances in home care are already making it possible for people with chronic illnesses to continue living and working from home. The design of some homes in this book enables a spouse, parent, or sibling to manage a chronic illness from home without giving up a career. Boomers are perhaps the first

generation that will benefit from telemedicine and telepharmacy. Telemedicine is a system that permits chronically ill patients to be monitored from home using e-mail, text-messaging, web-cam, and more. Houses can be equipped with sensors to monitor falls in a kitchen or bath and with robotic help with physical therapy or activities of daily living. Telepharmacy enables doctors to keep track of medications, or send prescriptions to the pharmacy.

Home can also heal in non-Western ways. Some of environments in this book are focused upon space for meditation and spirituality; one, known as Bioscleave is based upon the idea that unexpected twists and turns, textured floors, and angled walls can reverse the "destiny" of decline.

In the Company of Friends

Hundreds of like-minded boomers are relocating, sometimes far from larger cities or towns, to settings where they can enjoy a sport or a lifestyle, along with like-minded friends and neighbors. The blogger Ellen Brandt refers to thematic boomer communities as "intentional utopias" because they attract people who want to share a common dream, goal, or cause. Some thematic Boomer communities are religious, others are "green," and some revolve around a life of golf, tennis, skiing, or sailing. Many such places are almost communal in spirit. Brandt documents two experimental boomer "utopias," one planned around a vineyard and its cultivation by the group and the other designed for a group of small-business owners who want to live in adjoining townhouses, in apartments located above their shops or restaurants. Plans for a gay community called BOOM in Palm Springs, with houses designed by noted architects such as Diller Scofidio + Renfro and Joel Sanders, have recently been announced.

Some boomers are exploring the feasibility of cohousing, in which like-minded people form and sometimes actually build a community of their own. At this point, most cohousing in the United States is either multi-generational or for seniors. In fact, one of the architects interviewed for this book is about to retire to Silver Sage, senior cohousing community in Colorado. There are no boomer cohousing communities yet, but Ellen Freudenheim finds that cohousing is an "appealing model" that could catch on very soon:

> But imagine if millions of Boomers created new cohousing communities, committed to eating meals together in a common space, and committed to everyone pitching into managing the affairs of the community. People could remain in their own homes, rather than relocating either to a retirement community or living with extended families or, worst case, in old age institutions. It's an appealing model. Stay tuned, Boomers: cohousing may be the wave of the future.

Ageless Homes for Later Life

Boomers will be moving into later life with more years of education and more technological savvy than any generation thus far. According to The Boomer Project, boomers reject "one-size fits all" solutions. Even as adults, they are still anti status quo, especially when it comes to health, beauty, and fitness.

This translates into home design that must integrate style and geriatrics. Boomers *are* aware of home safety, but they are also willing to take some risks, and to defy conventional wisdom in the same of style and convenience.

We interviewed an architect who designed the "next stage" home for a semi-retired physician, whose specialty was geriatric medicine. He specifically wanted a two-story home with switchback stairs connecting the levels. The architect reported that the client had wisely installed grab bars in the shower and a universally designed kitchen, but he had insisted on the stairs. When asked about that decision, this geriatric physician said, "Going up and down the stairs may be the only exercise I get someday. I will need those stairs to stay in shape!"

We call these "Ageless Homes for Later Life" because they are an exciting mix of conventional geriatric design and ageless planning: homes that deliberately ignore or sidestep the conventional wisdom of design for senior housing. Many Boomers are aware that they will need everything from grab bars in showers to ergonomically designed kitchens, which will certainly help them to age in place. And they are taking advantage of products and technologies to make their homes safer. But they are also using space, light, energy, and color in unexpected ways.

Affordable But Never Boring

In the wake of the financial crisis, people in their early sixties who lave lost jobs or pensions or both are revisiting their retirement plans. Some are scaling back on the size, cost, and location of the homes where they might live. Fortunately, there is a new breed of affordable homes, townhouses, and condominiums that are handsomely designed and sustainable. Some of the "new" affordable housing has been designed to *create* community, and some has been designed to restore or revitalize a community. This new wave of housing is attractive for many reasons:

apart from being affordable, it is often green, sustainable, and downright welcoming.

Perhaps the most exciting *and* affordable single-family homes can be found in New Orleans, rising from the wreckage of the Lower 9th Ward. Brad Pitt's nonprofit Make It Right Foundation has worked with world-renowned architects to design green and affordable single-family homes that are now. attracting three-generation families, often headed by people in their early sixties.

On January 1, 2011, Dan Barry of the *New York Times* acknowledged the milestone of the first boomers turning sixty-five:

> On New Year's Day, the oldest members of the Baby Boom Generation will turn 65, the age once linked to retirement, early bird specials and gray Velcro shoes that go with everything . . . According to the Pew Research Center, for the next 19 years, about 10,000 people "will cross that threshold" every day—and many of them, whether through exercise or Botox, have no intention of ceding to others what they consider rightfully youth.

How boomers will fare over the next decades is unknown. What is certain is that the energy and determination that has served them so well will carry them forward to meet the challenges ahead.

REFERENCES

Andreen, Rick. "Boomers Want It Green." *JWT Live Wire* Winter 2009: 6–7.

Araton, Harvey. "When Home Shrinks." *New York Times*, 9 September 2009, home & garden section, p. 1.

Barry, Dan. "Boomers Hit New Self-Absorption Milestone: Age 65." *New York Times*, January 1, 2011.

Boomer Project. "Aging: By The Numbers." In *Longevity Rules: How To Age Well Into The Future*, edited by Stuart Greenbaum, 7–24. Carmichael, Calif.: Eskaton, 2010.

Boomer Project. "Reasons to Believe." In *Longevity Rules*, 217–35.

Jones, Finn-Olaf. "The Spirit Moved Them." *New York Times*, 28 December 2007, sec. F, p. F1.

Brandt, Ellen. "Back to Sophisticated Communes: Will Baby Boomers Come Full Circle?" *Angriest Generation*, 18 August 2009. AngriestGeneration.Wordpress.com/2009/08/18/back-to-sophisticated-communes.

Bremier, P.J. "Under The Living Roof: A Tiered, Extended-Family Design." *Marin Magazine* March 2009: 1–2.

Bretos, Conchy. "As the Boomers Will Tell You, It Takes A Village." *JWT Live Wire* Winter 2009: 4.

Dickinson, Elizabeth Evitts. "Old Age, New Models." *Architect* September 2008: 1.

Freudenheim, Ellen. "Baby Boomers May Change the Paradigm of Aging and Build Communities." *Suite101*, 30 September 2009. Suite101.com.

Gallagher, Winifred. *House Thinking: A Room-by-Room Look at How We Live*. New York: HarperCollins, 2006.

Kephart, Mike. "Small Niches Mean Big Business." *JWT LiveWire* Winter 2009: 10.

Mitchell, Jan. "Top Trends in 50+ Housing." *JWT Live Wire* Winter 2009: 14–16.

Nyren, Chuck. "Selling Universal Design to Baby Boomers." *TheMatureMarket.com*, 6 May 2006. www.TheMatureMarket.com.

Schulman, Ken. "Not Your Grandmother's Old Age." *Metropolis Magazine* December 2001: 1.

Toyota, Brian. "Building For Boomers." *ML Design*, 4 March 2008. http://www.mldesign.com.au/media/27.htm.

Viladas, Pilar. "Family Planning for Three Generations." *Design & Living* Winter 2009: 52–56.

Weigelt, David, and Jonathan Boehman. *Dot Boom: Marketing to Baby Boomers Through Meaningful Online Engagement*. Great Falls, Va.: Linx, 2009.

Zimmerman, Eilene. "How to make the best of a delayed retirement." *New York Times*, 5 July 2009, p. 16.

BISTRO LIVING: DOWNSIZED FOR VITALITY

After years of mowing lawns and shoveling snow, many boomers dream about leaving suburbia and trying something different. Some are taking advantage of retirement to explore the pleasures of city life. They are moving to apartments, townhouses, lofts, condominiums, or studios.

The desire for elegant, urbane living has kept surprisingly large numbers of boomers from relocating to planned communities. It explains the decision to sell a big suburban home or apartment and downsize to a smaller space in or near the city; something just as upscale as a suburban home, but easier to maintain.

Bistro living is an emerging lifestyle in metropolitan areas from New York to Des Moines. It continues to gain popularity among boomers who relish the freedom of the empty nest and want easy access to gyms, restaurants, shops, and museums. They relocate to residences that are often just a few miles from where they had lived before they retired and before the kids were grown.

One reason for this increase in bistro living is that large American cities have become safer in recent years. Crime is down. New York City, for example, signed onto the WHO Age-Friendly Cities project (2007), and it is doing everything possible to enable its residents to comfortably age in place. At the same time, cities continue to be magnets for the arts, fine cuisine, culture, and sports.

Jirsa Loft

Des Moines, Iowa

Jirsa Loft was built on the seventh floor of a reno-vated warehouse in a section of the city that was once in decline but is now an easy walk to res-taurants, athletic fields, and shopping. Like many other American cities, Des Moines is becoming a hub for culture, sports, health care, and fine dining.

The plan layout is diverse enough to offer the owner a variety of experiences. The public living areas are very open and lofty, but "in-between" spaces are more intimate and contemplative. In many of the rooms, entire walls of windows provide an expansive view of the city skyline. The refined and highly finished collection of living spaces—kitchen, media room, dining room, and bed-room—stand in contrast to the more raw industrial perimeter of the space.

ABOVE The owner of this loft in a newly gentrified area of Des Moines is a doctor who downsized from a larger house. The neighborhood offers culture, fine dining, and access to parks and social services.

BELOW Wide partitions and a neutral palette provide a handsome setting for a collection of contemporary works on paper. Generous open-ings and the combination of large areas of carpet-ing and smooth concrete flooring are part of the minimalist aesthetic and also look ahead to future needs.

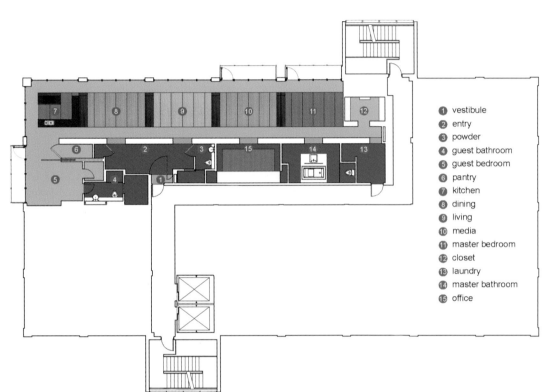

1 vestibule
2 entry
3 powder
4 guest bathroom
5 guest bedroom
6 pantry
7 kitchen
8 dining
9 living
10 media
11 master bedroom
12 closet
13 laundry
14 master bathroom
15 office

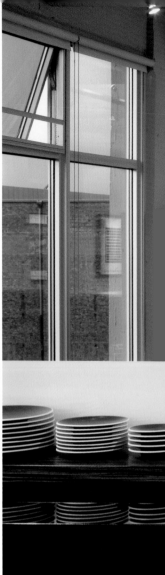

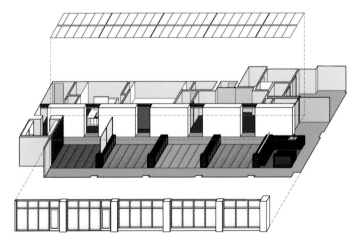

ABOVE The living space is partitioned with ebony dividers corresponding to the window bays. At the kitchen, a panel conceals countertop storage of tableware. Small, well-designed spaces are also ideal for aging in place because they put everything within easy reach.

BELOW The screen in the media area retracts into the ceiling; in the dining area, red leather chairs contrast with the glass table.

The loft accommodates a full range of activities, with an office and a handsome master suite. The downtown location allows a bicycle to replace a car for local transportation.

Kastan Loft

New York, New York

Designed for a boomer couple, the Kastan loft in west midtown Manhattan is a former parking garage. The husband is a psychiatrist, and the wife is a photographer's representative who works from home. She needed an office as well as a variety of flexible gallery arrangements for displaying photographs.

The couple had lived in New York for many years and were looking for a place to accommodate their evolving lifestyle that would be centrally located near Lincoln Center, the Time Warner Center, and other cultural landmarks. While creating a space where they could age in place, they made few concessions to gerontological features; a stairway leads to her office on the upper level (which in turn opens up onto a roof terrace).

Smaller stairs to the dining and media room don't currently have railings, but they could be added. Similarly, bathroom walls have been reinforced for future grab bars.

Project completed with Margaret Chapman.

The loft is in the up-and-coming Clinton area west of the theater district in Manhattan. The space was designed with multiple low changes of level as well as a stair leading to a roof terrace, reflecting the boomer attitude that the more you do, the more you can do. Ramps and even an elevator can be added if required.

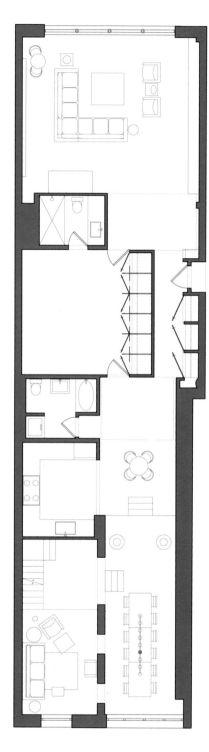

The loft is a renovated parking garage and retains some industrial elements. The study to the right of the dining room is the former auto elevator shaft.

A neutral palette of cream, white, and gray is used in the living room and master suite. A custom bookcase in the living room houses a collection of art reference books.

Walls in the entry hall and living
room function as gallery space.

Arthouse

Dallas, Texas

Most of the residents of this 8-unit condominium complex are boomers in their fifties and sixties. The building was conceived as single unified structure as opposed to the town house units that are more typical of the neighborhood. The design gives the units a sense of both privacy and community. The entrance, which includes a ramp, is through a covered canopy with an adjoining garden. An elevator takes residents from the on-grade parking to the second level, which is anchored by a two-story atrium open to the sky. The entrances to the units are from this space, which also provides internal natural light.

Like so many boomers, this working professional chose an apartment that would put him near the cultural and social life of Dallas, and, at the same time, provide a sheltered and peaceful setting.

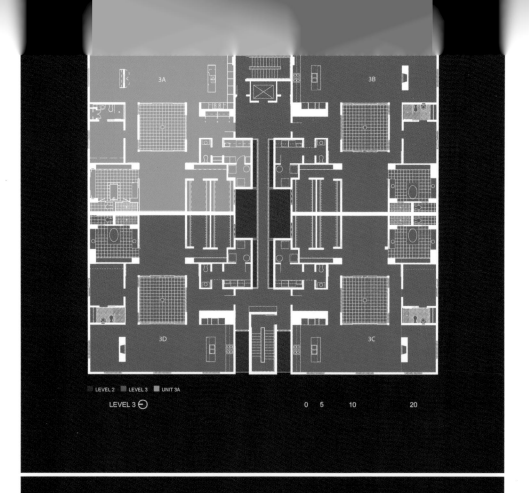

3A 3B

3D 3C

■ LEVEL 2 ■ LEVEL 3 ■ UNIT 3A

LEVEL 3 ⊖   0 5 10 20

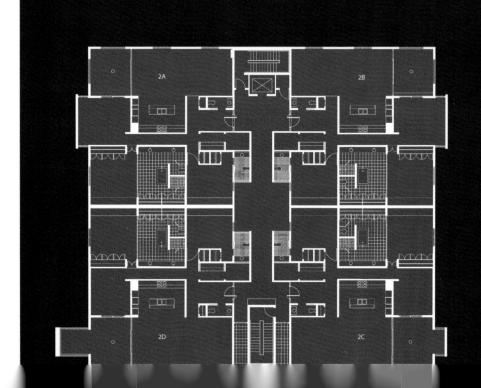

2A 2B

2D 2C

The apartments are
on the second and
third floors, above
the parking, which
affords privacy and

Wide doorways and open spaces will make it possible for the owner to age in place. The central atrium provides natural light, while the natural wood adds welcome warmth to the minimalist design.

The Hollywood

Los Angeles, California

The Hollywood condominium is a fifty-four-unit building with a courtyard that serves as the social core for the complex. This central space is anchored by an indoor pool, which gives the sense of a high-end hotel—a hallmark of bistro living.

The units have lofty seventeen-foot ceilings and an open, flexible plan. Recessed balconies and floor-to-ceiling windows offer sweeping views of Hollywood. These apartments are near a huge shopping and entertainment complex that houses the famed Kodak Theatre, with easy access to cultural activities.

The pool is the focal point of the social life of the complex.

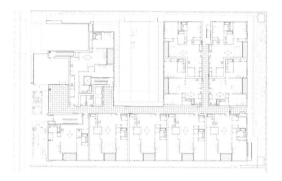

1ST FLOOR PLAN

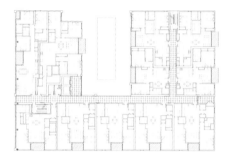

4TH FLOOR PLAN

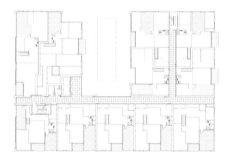

5TH FLOOR MEZZANINE PLAN

5TH FLOOR PLAN

A lively rhythm of windows animates the facade and ensures that each apartment is unique.

Public spaces are
designed specifically
for residents to
mingle. Each
apartment offers
a panoramic view
of downtown Los
Angeles.

The rich brown and
white palette creates
an sophisticated
interior setting.

THREE GENERATIONS TOGETHER: MULTIFAMILY HOMES AND COMMUNITIES

According to folk wisdom, "It takes a village to raise a child," but most boomers do not have that option. Many working couples in need of childcare have turned instead to their own parents. Of course, this is nothing new. The difference today is that more families are interested in living in three-generational homes or communities. These are not "accessory homes" as much as organic designs for housing three generations together.

Boomers will be the first generation in the United States to reach age sixty-five with one or both parents in good health. Some are not so fortunate, however. A survey from Campbell-Ewald Health shows an estimated thirteen million boomers are caregivers for frail parents or in-laws.

But today, more than ever before, older people are in good health and committed to being actively involved with their grandchildren. They often want to live close enough to enjoy them and participate in their upbringing. This requires homes designed for family life rather than settings for geriatric care.

The following examples show how houses can promote intergenerational linkages. Two were actually developed at the insistence of grandparents who wanted to live near children and grandchildren. The third example is a multigenerational community, designed foster feelings of kinship among residents of all ages. Amenities include preschool playgrounds, a senior center, and a place for teenagers to hang out. Although most of the people who live there are technically not family members, they report feeling closely connected to their friends and neighbors on this three-generational campus.

Architecturally, all of these projects offer both community and privacy and solitude. Together, they show that increased longevity can be a bonus for all members of the family, and the basis for forward-looking design. This is unassisted living in the true sense of that phrase.

Mill Valley House

Mill Valley, California

Architect Scott McGlashan worked with a family that craved the proximity of grandparents and grandchildren, but was unable to arrive at a workable design for housing the three generations. They originally wanted to create a compound containing three separate houses: one for the grandparents, one for the married son and his children, and one for the married daughter and her children. Eventually, they settled on a design that would keep the son and his family in the property's existing house, and would locate the daughter's family and the grandparents in a nearby three-story tiered house.

The result is a home for grandparents, two married children, and all of their kids. It is solar powered, with green roofs, among other sustainable features. An added bonus: the houses are designed so that the married children can also age in place.

An extended family—a couple, their son and daughter-in-law, their daughter and son-in-law, and their grandchildren—lives in this three-tiered structure.

EAST (ENTRY) ELEVATION

0 5 10 15 FT

273

GARDEN

UPPER FLOOR

SHARED FLOOR

DRIVEWAY

DECK

PATIO

PARKING

LOWER FLOOR

DECK

SITE PLAN

0 10 20 30 FT

The different levels
house distinct family
units, while the out-
door spaces serve to
unify them. The result-
ing home provides
specific territory for
each household and
also defines them as
an extended family.

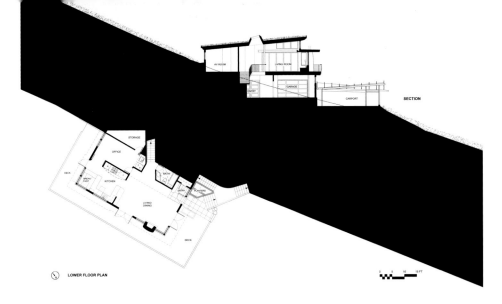

SECTION

AV ROOM

LIVING ROOM

GARAGE

ENTRY

CARPORT

STORAGE

OFFICE

DECK

BREAK-FAST

KITCHEN

BATH

ENTRY

PLANTERS

LIVING/ DINING

DECK

LOWER FLOOR PLAN

0   5   10   15 FT

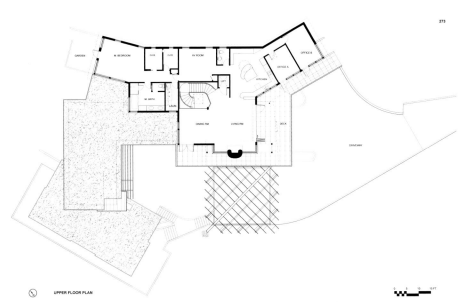

273

UTILITIES/STORAGE

LIFT

PLANTER

ENTRY HALL

BEDROOM

AWAY ROOM

BATH

BEDROOM

GARAGE

BATH

CLOS.

PLANTER

BEDROOM

GARDEN

PARKING

SHARED FLOOR PLAN

0   5   10   15 FT

273

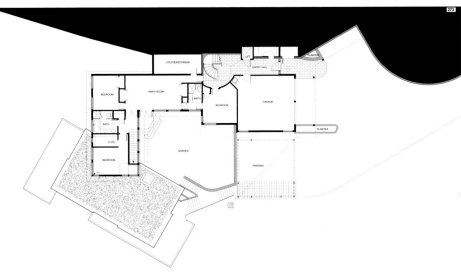

GARDEN

M. BEDROOM

CLOS.

CLOS.

AV ROOM

OFFICE A

OFFICE B

KITCHEN

LIFT

M. BATH

LAUN.

DINING RM

LIVING RM

DECK

DRIVEWAY

Folding doors add
flexibility and the
option of connecting
indoors and out.
Flexible space is
especially important
for extended families
where roles and
relationships shift
throughout the day.

UPPER FLOOR PLAN

0   5   10   15 FT

The house is designed
to be sustainable and
solar-powered, with
green roofs for insulation
and water conservation
at each tier.

Private Residence

Shelburne, Vermont

TruexCullins and landscape designer Keith Wagner Partnership worked to create a place where a boomer couple could live with their daughter and her two children. This multigenerational space consists of two homes, one for the grandparents and the other for their daughter's family. The grandparents, who lived further south, originally wanted a second home where they could spend their summers. However, they quickly decided that proximity to their grandchildren, and the magnificent views of Lake Champlain, were worth relocating for. According to architect Rolf Kielman, the volumes of the two houses were designed to frame the lake and at the same time to connect the three generations.

Kielman recalls that he, along with the landscape architect and the grandparents, first visited this lakeside property during the winter (on snowshoes) and did their preliminary sketches in the snow. Those finger marks, explains Kielman, became the basis for the architecture and landscaping of this lakeside property.

The front doors of two separate but adjacent houses face each other across an entry porch.

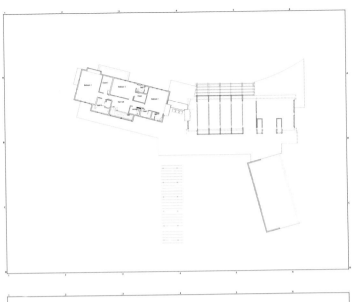

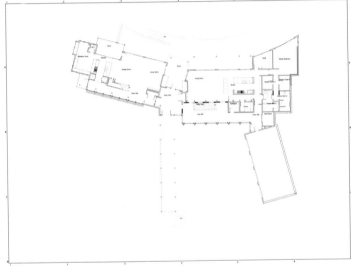

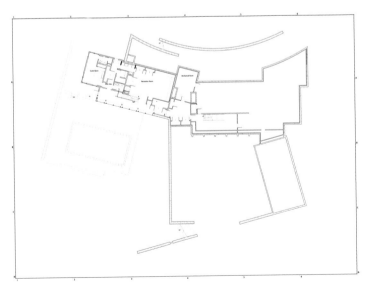

The landscape is sculpted to create privacy for each household and to provide easy access from one house to the other. For now, the adjacency allows the grandparents to help their daughter with childcare. Eventually this arrangement could just as easily allow her to look after her aging parents.

The main living area is spacious enough for all three generations in this "refilled nest."

Taube Koret Campus for Jewish Life

Palo Alto, California

This pedestrian-friendly intergenerational campus offers independent housing, assisted living, and senior affordable housing. Facilities include a state-of-the-art sports and wellness center, indoor and outdoor pools, and the Leslie Family Early Childhood Education Center. There are also meeting rooms and spaces for adult, senior, teen, and youth programs.

The architects designed the campus with multiple places to gather and stroll. "We wanted this to be an active place, a walking place," Robert Steinberg says. By being walkable and open, Taube Koret creates and sustains linkages between generations. Some of these connections are programmed, as when seniors are invited to participate in activities at the preschool. But the campus also makes it easy for people of all ages to come together spontaneously, as when older residents take their grandchildren into the warm-water pool or have a snack with a friend or family member. While Taube Koret is ideal for three-generation families, it also has the larger mission of creating connections among people who become neighbors and friends because they live there.

A winding central walking street (the Midrash) connects distinct activity centers for seniors, teens, and children in this multi-generational community.

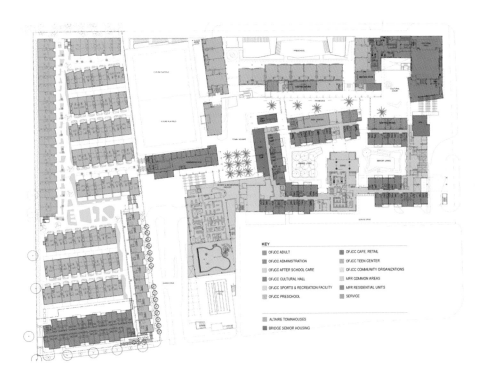

The living and social areas of Taube Koret are visually connected and encourage the feeling of a multi-generational community, while providing separate space and activity areas for each generation.

GETAWAYS

Some boomers are planning their getaway home by making a beach house or lakeside cabin into a retirement spot. This makes good sense, in that most getaways are scenic and serene, or located near activities that can finally become full-time passions.

All of the homes featured in this chapter are getaways where it will be possible to age in place. The first is the classic example of a beach house that is more than two hours away from the owner's main residence. The other two projects are getaways, but with a twist: both of them are just a stone's throw away from the main house, but they seem like they are worlds away.

ROBERT M. GURNEY

Lujan House

Ocean View, Delaware

This house with views of the Chesapeake Bay was designed for a woman who loves the outdoors but had to build her getaway on a budget. Though Lujan House looks spacious, it is actually a compact residence on a small piece of land. The house appears larger because it is U-shaped, which also maximizes the views of the bay.

It is a low-maintenance home of corrugated metal and concrete block, with natural groundcover instead of lawns that would need to be watered and mowed. Zoned heating gives the flexibility to use space selectively. The master suite is a focal point; another wing contains two guest rooms for visits from grandchildren and friends.

A budget-friendly getaway today, the house is destined to be a full-time residence when the owner retires. She will wake up to years of water views when she finally relocates there.

The generous living space is divided into three zones; a large rug helps distinguish the seating area from the dining space and kitchen.

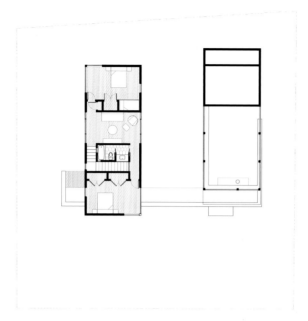

SECOND FLOOR PLAN

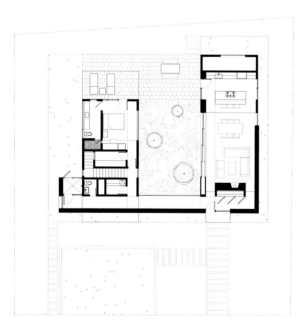

FIRST FLOOR PLAN

The outdoor paving
surface is smooth
enough to accom-
modate future use of
mobility devices.

ABOVE The kitchen combines a high level of design with low maintenance through the use of long countertops and natural materials

RIGHT The long corridor has a minimum of glare and is intentionally uncluttered.

Deck House

Austin, Texas

As architect Rosa Rivera recalls, her clients wanted a weekend retreat in their own backyard. The result is the Deck House, which is just a hundred yards away from the main house.

The clients are married professionals with college-aged children who realized that they now had more time. But they are passionate about living in Austin. Rivera, also an Austin resident, understands this completely. "People in Austin refuse to grow old," she says. Rivera helped to keep them young by designing a flexible, detached addition to their home.

Deck House gives this family the best of two worlds. On weekends they are able to leave the main house but still stay close to the city lights of Austin. In the future, when they retire, they will be able to move without really moving.

Clear glass railings on the deck do not obstruct the panoramic view but are strong enough to prevent slips or falls. The outdoor furniture is stable and comfortable for all ages.

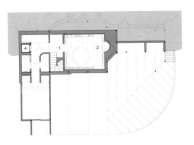

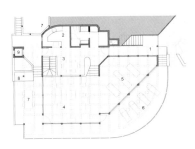

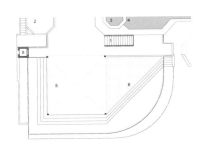

Cellar Level

3m
0' 4' 10'

1 Foyer to Lower Level
2 Wine Cellar
3 Bedroom
4 Elevator

Lower Level Plan

3m
0' 4' 10'

1 Entry
2 Kitchen
3 Dining
4 Lounge
5 Gym
6 West Deck
7 Outdoor Dining
8 Barbecue
9 Elevator

Upper Deck Plan

3m
0' 4' 10'

1 Entry to Lower Level
2 Overlook
3 Existing Spa
4 Existing Pool
5 Fabric structure above
6 Deck
7 Deck below
8 Elevator

ABOVE LEFT Deck House is
perched at the top of the bluff.

ABOVE RIGHT The entrance
threshold has no level change and is
wide enough for mobility devices.

OPPOSITE Low pathway lights
make it easier to navigate garden
steps at night.

The deck offers a
panoramic view of
the Texas landscape.

GRAY ORGANSCHI ARCHITECTURE

COTTAGE

Guilford, Connecticut

A retired couple in Connecticut had planned to convert a dilapidated cottage on their property into a freestanding library and writer's corner, but instead they decided to demolish it and build something in its place. They were so charmed by its replacement—an airy, shedlike structure with a lofted sleeping area, large sliding windows, and magnificent views of Long Island Sound—that they made it their getaway.

Sustainable features include a ground-source heat pump and a sod roof. It is possible to stand on the deck, made from FSC-certified ipe, and enjoy a view that would never have been possible from the previous cottage on that site. The couple now spend so much time in the new cottage that it may be tempting to ignore the main house, which is just a few hundred feet away.

The cottage is oriented to minimize glare from the expanses of glass that provide abundant natural light and open views.

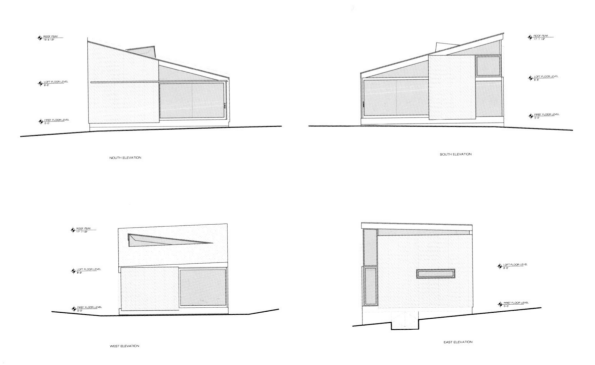

NORTH ELEVATION

SOUTH ELEVATION

WEST ELEVATION

EAST ELEVATION

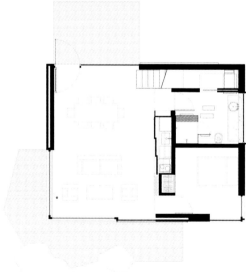

0   5   10ft.

The glass and cedar-clad cottage
is just a short walk from the
main house, but it looks and
feels worlds away. The owners
specified sustainable features
like the sod roof.

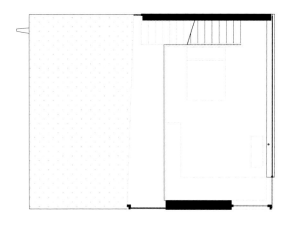

0   5   10ft.

ABOVE LEFT A loft space overlooks the double-height dining room.

ABOVE RIGHT When the house was photographed, the stairway was freestanding, but supports and banisters have now been added.

OPPOSITE Pendant lighting adds a soft overhead glow, minimizing glare by day and providing primary lighting after dark.

OFF THE GRID: LATER LIFE IN WIDE OPEN SPACES

Boomers are the first generation to take advantage of breakthroughs in technology to live wherever they please in later life. Some of them are settling in isolated places: on a ranch, perched upon a rugged bluff, in the bayou, or fifty feet from a river in the middle of a redwood forest.

Unlike the getaways in the previous chapter, these are not weekend retreats. They are permanent homes. Despite their remote locations, they are well designed and architecturally interesting. They are technologically sophisticated as well, since these boomers and their families depend on technology to remain connected to their careers, health care, and relatives and friends while living off the grid.

All of the homes in this chapter are sustainable, but they do not feel like campsites. They are filled with amenities that have less to do with survival than with gracious living: swimming pools, gym areas, guest suites, and in one case a patio that can accommodate a small chamber orchestra. With the exception of the compact Corum Residence, they all include guest accommodations.

This is not Walden! All of these houses are for married couples and their families. "Off the grid" does not mean solitude. Boomers may want to live in wide open spaces, but they do not want to be alone in later life.

CORUM RESIDENCE

Pella, Iowa

A boomer couple wanted to simplify life by downsizing and putting more distance between themselves and their neighbors. They had read James Gauer's book *The New American Dream: Living Well In Small Spaces* and took the author's message to heart. The result was Corum Residence. It is isolated, private, and compact, without an inch of wasted space anywhere.

The couple's two children have bedrooms on the lower level. Upstairs is a loftlike master bedroom that "borrows" sunlight from the windows below since the couple felt it would be wasteful to have any windows in the loft.

The house shows that it is possible to downsize and move "down-grid" without compromising on style or function. The home is as private and no-nonsense as the family that lives there. But it is well designed and elegant. Its compact design makes Corum Residence ideal spot for this couple to age in place.

The lofted master bedroom offers privacy for the parents. Two bedroom on the lower level are currently used by their children, but could someday be converted into space for an aging parent or for a caregiver.

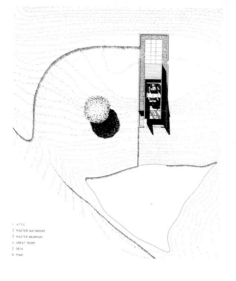

1 ATTIC
2 MASTER BATHROOM
3 MASTER BEDROOM
4 GREAT ROOM
5 DECK
6 POND

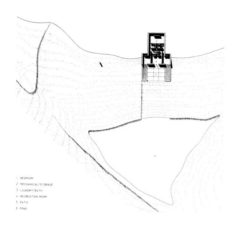

1 BEDROOM
2 MECHANICAL/STORAGE
3 LAUNDRY/BATH
4 RECREATION ROOM
5 PATIO
6 POND

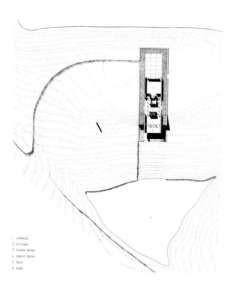

1 GARAGE
2 KITCHEN
3 DINING ROOM
4 GREAT ROOM
5 DECK
6 POND

Like many boomers, this couple wanted to minimize energy costs in later life. Large windows function in a passive solar manner as a source of heat and light. In addition, they make the compact space feel light and airy.

Interior finishes
are natural and
practical for easy
maintenance.

Spicewood **Residence**

Spicewood, Texas

The client had spent his entire career as a surgeon in Dallas, where he did painstakingly delicate procedures in windowless operating rooms. His wife is an attorney. With one child in college and the other in law school, they decided it was time to retire and spend more time enjoying family and friends, hobbies, and nature.

An avid outdoorsman, the husband retired while he was still energetic enough for life full of camping, boating, and the wilderness. They built Spicewood on a bluff overlooking Lake Travis, in the Hill Country of East Texas. The home is ruggedly suited to the rough terrain on which it stands. Spicewood requires no outside water. It only uses rainwater runoff, which is collected in 20,000-gallon cisterns.

Spicewood may be high on a bluff, but that does not stop the couple who live there from entertaining family and friends. There is a guesthouse on the property, as well as a pool. Though Spicewood is off the grid, there is still room enough for frequent visitors.

Exterior materials—
rough calico limestone
and stucco—reflect
the rugged East Texas
landscape.

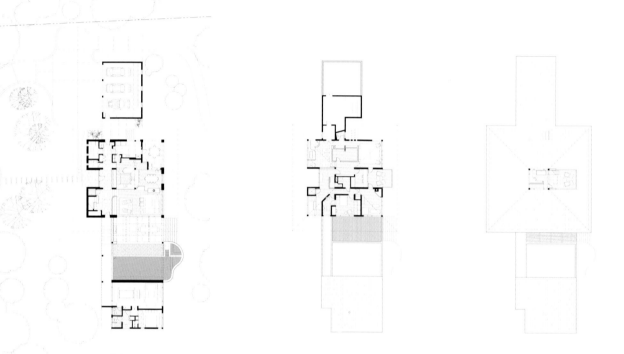

ABOVE Deep roof overhangs shade the facade, reducing the heat and glare of the Texas sunlight, while geothermal coils that displace heat into the ground eliminate the need for air conditioning condensing units.

RIGHT A covered walkway connects the main house to the guest house. The pool terrace between the two is a welcome place to catch the prevailing breeze from the lake below.

Spicewood sits on an isolated, rugged bluff,
but the owners never intended to leave family
and friends behind. The house may be off the
grid, but it provides comfortable spaces for
family gatherings and other social events.

Wyoming Canyon Ranch

Wyoming

Set within a remote mountain site, this house incorporates natural materials of stone, concrete, and wood with state of the art building systems and technologies. The terraces, generous glazing and indoor/outdoor spaces extend the living spaces into the dramatic landscape. The house is sensitively integrated into a naturally evolved protected area within the site. Open panoramic views from the great room frame the Bridger National Forest to the east, and an indoor/outdoor informal piano concert space to the west. The master suite was designed to capture both the mountain views and the experience of being nestled within an aspen grove.

The ranch has been in the owners' family for three generations. Currently the owners live here for part of the year, but when their children are grown, they intend to become permanent residents. Living quarters in the adjacent barn will allow independence for visiting adult children and ultimately become a space for the parents once the children occupy the main house.

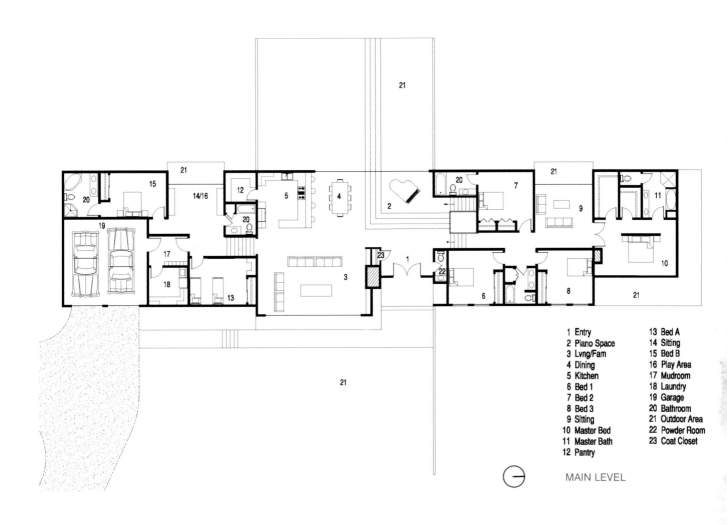

21

21

| 15 | 14/16 | 12 | 5 | 4 | 2 | 20 | 7 | 21 | 11 |
20 | 19 | 17 | 18 | 13 | 3 | 23 | 1 | 22 | 6 | 9 | 8 | 10

21

21

1 Entry
2 Piano Space
3 Lvng/Fam
4 Dining
5 Kitchen
6 Bed 1
7 Bed 2
8 Bed 3
9 Sitting
10 Master Bed
11 Master Bath
12 Pantry

13 Bed A
14 Sitting
15 Bed B
16 Play Area
17 Mudroom
18 Laundry
19 Garage
20 Bathroom
21 Outdoor Area
22 Powder Room
23 Coat Closet

MAIN LEVEL

The horizontal form
of the house follows
the contour of the
site and rests lightly
on the land.

LEFT Ample counter space and two sinks make the kitchen efficient for both family and formal occasions.

RIGHT A music space, on axis with the entrance and open to the view, allows the couple, both amateur musicians, to hold concerts for their friends. Like many later-life homes, this one satisfies the traditional urge to return to nature and the very contemporary need to remain connected to professional and personal activities and interests.

Riverbend Residence

North Bend, Washington

Sometimes moving off the grid is about "returning" rather than "running away." This house was built by a couple with two children who were living in downtown Seattle but needed something different. The husband and wife, who had both grown up outside the city, wanted to return to rural life. They built River Bend fifty feet from the Snoqualmie River in North Bend, Washington, and they plan to age in place there. They created a space where they would have twenty-first-century comfort while living on a five-acre site on a riverbank in the forest.

Inspired by fallen redwoods on the property, architect Chris Pardo designed a home that features horizontal planes of wood, concrete, and aluminum. The house provides a soothing space for a family that had grown tired of Seattle's traffic and urban buzz, and the design is as sustainable as the surrounding forest. A geothermal in-ground heat loop and Desuperheater heat water during the cooling season and reduce energy usage during the heating season.

The house was designed to be green and sustainable with minimal impact on the land.

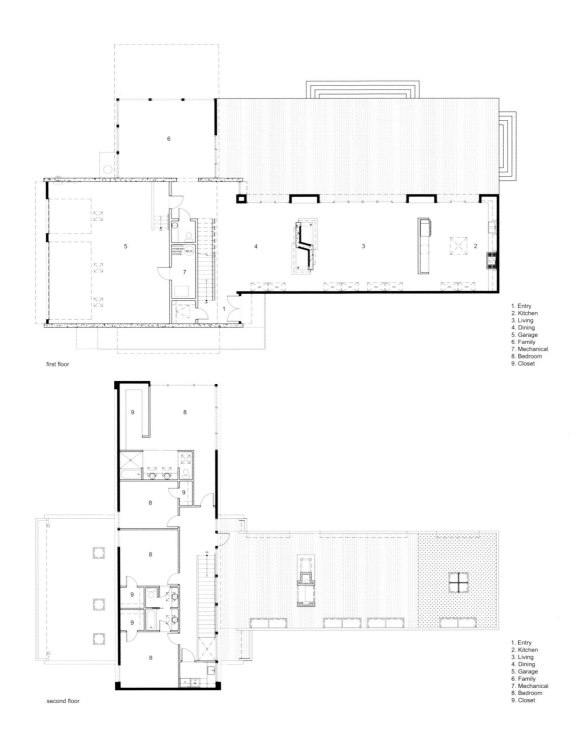

first floor

1. Entry
2. Kitchen
3. Living
4. Dining
5. Garage
6. Family
7. Mechanical
8. Bedroom
9. Closet

second floor

1. Entry
2. Kitchen
3. Living
4. Dining
5. Garage
6. Family
7. Mechanical
8. Bedroom
9. Closet

Natural light floods
the interior through
windows, skylights,
and sliding glass
doors. The sound
of the rushing river
pervades the space.

Conceived as three
masses (private,
living, service) and
three materials
(wood, concrete,
aluminum), the
house has a
low-maintenance
exterior.

WORKING AND HEALING FROM HOME

Home will be the nerve center for "ageless aging." Even before retirement, boomers have become accustomed to working from home, and they often insist they will continue as consultants or adjuncts after they retire. But working from home will put more demands on the home office. For many boomers, that room will become the primary spot to store information and materials needed for part-time work. In the absence of an outside workplace, even the most firmly retired boomers will need to create storage space and office space at home. One of the homes in this chapter anticipates another change that comes from losing office space: the lack of a conference room. The Barn Addition in Westport, Connecticut, doubles as both a home office and a space for meetings and salons (and yoga too). The home office at Bouldin Residence in Austin, Texas, serves two people, a married couple who both plan to keep working from home for many years to come.

Ageless aging might be a boomer ideal, but even for this health-and-fitness-focused generation, old age inevitably includes illness, injury, and management of chronic conditions (commonly called "self care"). Home will sometimes need to be a place of healing for physical ailments, along with the emotional stresses they cause. Some illnesses are progressive and will need to be closely monitored from home. The boomer passion for sports and fitness pretty much guarantees that they will also spend some time recovering from related injuries at home.

There is already an array of literature on boomers who are preparing to care for older parents or in-laws. It serves a reminder that boomers—even the most "ageless" of them—will eventually have to heal themselves.

ARTISTS HOME AND STUDIOS

Southampton, New York

This is a house for a married couple who wanted a place where they could work near each other and grow older together. The husband and wife are both artists, each with a distinctive style and creative process. For this reason, they decided to build separate studios for themselves, alongside the home and sculpted pool that David Barrett designed for them in Southampton.

They sought out Barrett because he shares their interest in green design, and he incorporated ecofriendly features such as geothermal heating and cooling. This a home where the couple can celebrate the environment, make art, and relish the changing seasons.

Both studios are accommodated in a building adjacent to the house. Clerestory windows provide ample natural light.

The curved roofs of the main house
contrast with the angular form
of the studio. Both address the
sculpted swimming pool, which
was designed by the owner. Home
and work are balanced by and
reflected in this swimming pool.

The wife is also a color theorist. She has used more than forty shades of color to create plane and volume throughout the house.

ROBERT M. GURNEY

Buisson Residence

Lake Anna, Virginia

The owners are retired but continue working from their home. In discussions with architect Robert Gurney, they concluded that the home office had to be integral to the design of Buisson Residence, not just an afterthought. "They didn't want to relegate the office to the basement," Gurney recalls. Since the couple wanted the workspace to be something special, he designed a double-height home office that overlooks a lake and features Brazilian cherry wood flooring and beech cabinetry.

The house is on the small side but suffices because it provides well-defined and well-crafted spaces for work, dining, and entertaining. There is one eating space, which is casual but elegant, and guest rooms for weekends when children and grandchildren visit. Buisson Residence makes it easy for this couple to share a rich, vibrant life together, as they continue working, grandparenting, and entertaining.

The house is zoned to allow the owners to work in the home office on the second floor while children, grandchildren, and guests enjoy the living space below. There is space for an elevator, should it become difficult to climb the stairs.

Abundant glazing
provides expansive
views of the lake and
the landscape.

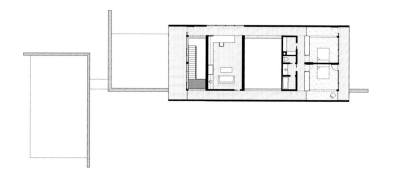

SECOND FLOOR PLAN

0   10   20   30

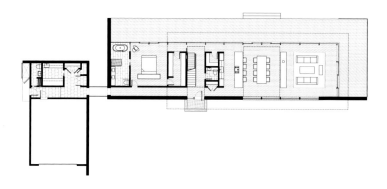

FIRST FLOOR PLAN

0   10   20   30

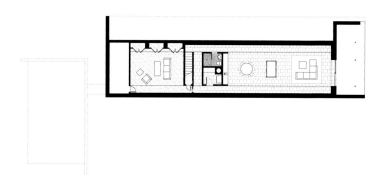

GROUND FLOOR PLAN

N   0   10   20   30

The great room
is divided into
living areas by low
partitions that also
function as storage.
A double-sided
fireplace serves both
living and dining
spaces.

JAMES B. WEIL

Weil Barn Addition

Westport, Connecticut

As James B. Weil tells it, he first saw the barn in 2005, fell in love with the post and beams, and knew instantly that they should be part of his home. The challenge was to transport it from Wethersfield, Vermont, to his home in Westport, Connecticut. The barn was disassembled in November and transported in pieces on a flatbed to Westport. The pieces were reassembled there over five days. No nails were used, only pegs.

On his own, Weil had researched woods, insulation options, geothermal and solar companies, and more. The barn was finally joined to Weil's home in 2006, in time for his daughter's wedding.

It has become a tranquil multipurpose space. Almost from the start, the barn addition became a space for yoga, meditation, work, meetings, and dinner parties. Now that he is retired, Weil appreciates that he can continue to grow professionally and spiritually in this remarkable space. The addition is an authentic example of space where this boomer can continue to work and heal from home.

The addition of clerestory lighting makes this rustic space more functional as a home office and conference room.

Built of reclaimed
materials and
producing energy
from solar panels
and geothermal
wells, the barn is a
sustainable space.

The symmetry of
the barn gives it the
flexibility to be a work
or meditation space
today, but it could also
be used as a class-
room or corporate
retreat if the owner's
interests change.

Bouldin Residence

Austin, Texas

Bouldin is home to a married couple who moved to Austin from a large city in the northeast and are involved in Austin's thriving music scene. Like many boomers, they continue to be involved with their careers and with the music industry. With the help of architect Kevin Alter, they created a sustainable home where they can remain connected to their work and entertain clients or friends.

The largest room is the upstairs office, which occupies half the second floor and stretches the full length of the house. There is a 9-by-9-foot media room downstairs, which allows the couple to work more easily from home. In addition to the media room, there is also a guest suite with a full bathroom on the first floor. Currently it is used when visitors stay over, but it could become the master suite if the couple ever need to live downstairs.

Bouldin has been oriented for optimal cross-ventilation and is outfitted for rainwater collection. The house also contains a solar photovoltaic array, solar pool heating tubes, reflective thermoplastic polyolefin roofing, and other energy-saving features. In choosing to make their home sustainable, they added features that would help them enjoy their work, their garden, and their pool for years to come.

The stairway leads to a commanding home office, which occupies half the space on the second floor.

FIRST FLOOR PLAN

SECOND FLOOR PLAN

N
0   15

1   entry
2   living
3   patio
4   kitchen
5   dining
6   laundry
7   mudroom
8   media
9   carport
10 pool
11 bedroom
12 office

There are two bedrooms on the second floor and a third on the ground floor, which can easily become the master suite. Sliding glass doors connect the kitchen and dining space to the patio and provide a dramatic view of a historic tree.

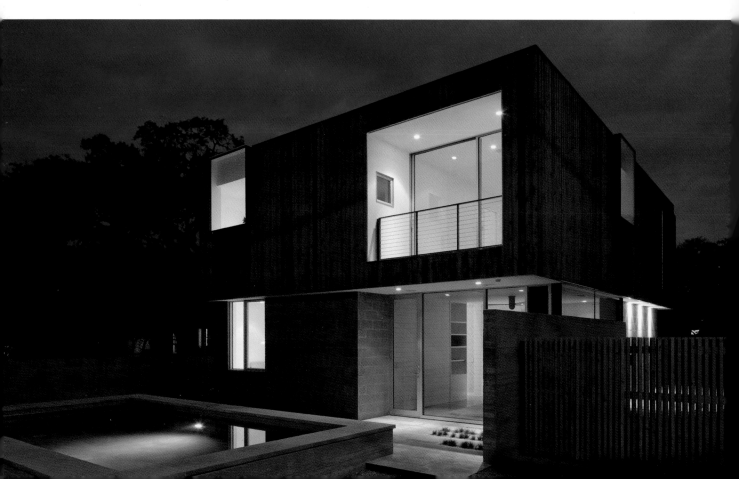

The interiors convey an exceptional discipline both in the materials and in the limited color palette with its bright yellow highlight.

Bioscleave House

East Hampton, New York

If ever there were a home for ageless aging, it would be Bioscleave House. Designed by Madeline Gins and Shusaku Arakawa, it embodied their abiding faith in the "reversible destiny" of life and home. Bioscleave is the latest in a series of houses designed to reverse the destiny of aging by making life more challenging and interesting.

Bioscleave provokes residents and visitors to be actively engaged with the living space. The color is vibrant, and the interior unfolds in a series of unpredictable twists, turns, and sloping spaces. Light switches and windows are never where one might expect them to be. The mere act of turning on the light should be an adventure, Arakawa and Gins insisted. And furthermore, life—and home—should be fun.

An environment for health and happiness, Bioscleave aspires to be much more than a place for healing. It was designed to actually do the healing.

Floor-to-ceiling poles of various colors act as supports and visual markers as people make their way across the room. Floors are intentionally textured to make walking across Bioscleave more of an "adventure."

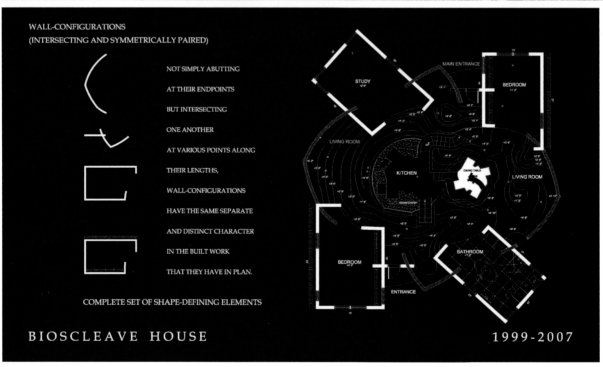

WALL-CONFIGURATIONS
(INTERSECTING AND SYMMETRICALLY PAIRED)

NOT SIMPLY ABUTTING

AT THEIR ENDPOINTS

BUT INTERSECTING

ONE ANOTHER

AT VARIOUS POINTS ALONG

THEIR LENGTHS,

WALL-CONFIGURATIONS

HAVE THE SAME SEPARATE

AND DISTINCT CHARACTER

IN THE BUILT WORK

THAT THEY HAVE IN PLAN.

COMPLETE SET OF SHAPE-DEFINING ELEMENTS

STUDY

MAIN ENTRANCE

BEDROOM

LIVING ROOM

KITCHEN

DINING TABLE

LIVING ROOM

COUNTERTOP

BEDROOM

BATHROOM

ENTRANCE

BIOSCLEAVE HOUSE

1999-2007

The grounds of
Bioscleave form an
intentional maze,
which makes every
stroll around the
grounds into a "way-
finding" exploration.

There are grab bars near
the shower and toilet in
the master suite. The goal
is to make this and every
room safe yet challenging
to the senses.

Luminous Bodies Residence

Vanderburgh County, Indiana

Architect Reginald Stump created Luminous Bodies as a home for his parents. Like Bioscleave, this is a house with an agenda: Luminous Bodies will allow the couple to live and work, despite his mother's progressive, chronic illness. The house anticipates and responds to the fact that the disease could worsen.

The name "Luminous Bodies" comes from the fact that one night, Stump drove his parents to the lot where he planned to build their home. He asked them to walk the land in the dark of night, with lights attached to their bodies. As he stood in the distance, all he could see were their illuminated forms. The lights showed his father's controlled, smooth gait and his mother's quick, spastic steps.

Building on this preliminary study, he created a safe and healing home for his parents. Luminous Bodies is all on one floor. There are no thresholds, very few doors (three in the entire house), and shelving within arm's reach in every room. According to Stump, the big V-shaped structural columns came about because his mother wants to keep the floor as clear and uncluttered as possible. The house gives his parents the space, confidence, and convenience to keep living there, even if his mother's physical condition declines.

With no thresholds and only three doors, the design facilitates ease of access and helps to prevent slips and falls.

OVERLEAF Apart from their dramatic appearance, the massive pairs of angled columns provide sturdy supports for somebody who might be unsteady on her feet.

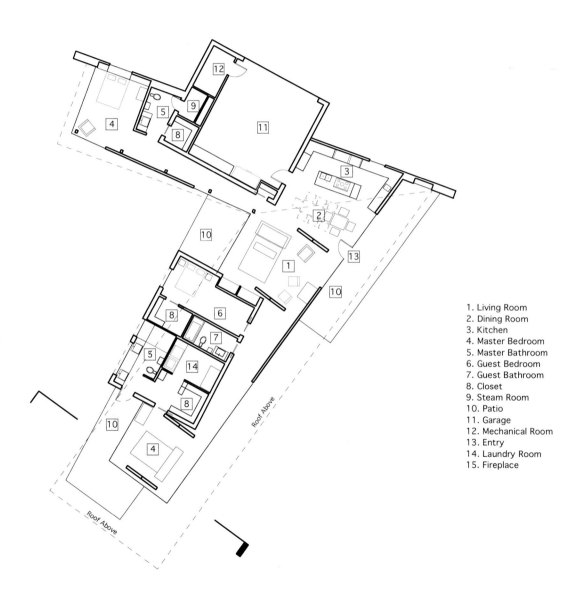

1. Living Room
2. Dining Room
3. Kitchen
4. Master Bedroom
5. Master Bathroom
6. Guest Bedroom
7. Guest Bathroom
8. Closet
9. Steam Room
10. Patio
11. Garage
12. Mechanical Room
13. Entry
14. Laundry Room
15. Fireplace

OPPOSITE ABOVE The spacing between the columns creates places to "rest" for a person with compromised mobility.

OPPOSITE BELOW A broad path leads to the entry, which is protected by the overhang of the roof.

OPPOSITE Furnishings are grouped to keep the floor uncluttered. The master bathroom is wide enough to accommodate a wheelchair, and the sink is raised to provide legroom.

ABOVE The storage unit in the bedroom is fitted with shelving behind doors, eliminating the pulling and pushing associated with drawers.

Emigration Canyon Residence

Salt Lake City, Utah

This single-family residence was designed to anticipate the necessity of caring for a frail relative. Nestled in Utah's Emigration Canyon north of Salt Lake City, the house is barrier-free and wheelchair accessible, in accordance with the principles of universal design.

The residence could easily accommodate a person with disabilities. All that would be needed is a ramp, which could be installed if necessary. The bathroom has space for a more user-friendly shower, should it become impossible to use the bathtub. The lower level of the house contains a separate guest suite and bathroom, which could easily be converted into quarters for a family member with disabilities or a caregiver.

This is the first LEED Silver certified residence in the state of Utah. But the house is not only sustainable and safe. It is also a place for family members to enjoy health, happiness, and one another.

The rectilinear form of the houses extends to the detailing of the fireplace and wood storage.

OVERLEAF
To make the house accessible, the rear entry steps can be converted to a ramp.

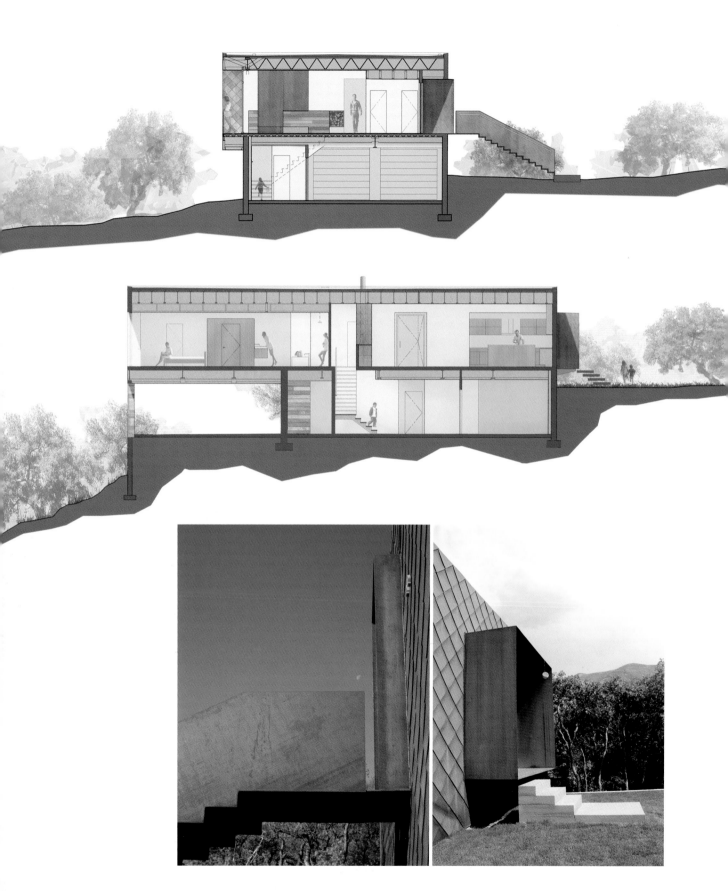

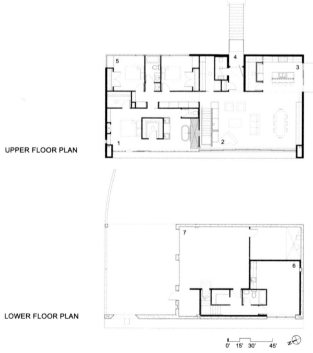

UPPER FLOOR PLAN

LOWER FLOOR PLAN

1 Master bedroom
2 Living Room
3 Kitchen
4 Entrance
5 Bedroom
6 Multipurpose Room
7 Garage

0' 15' 30' 45'

The kitchen, bedroom, and great room are all located on one level. The design anticipates the need for a wheel-chair-accessible interior. Furnishings have been arranged to maximize space for grandchildren to play, but also to provide easier mobility for those in walkers or wheelchairs. The bathroom is universally designed, with grips near the bathtub for added safety.

IN THE COMPANY OF FRIENDS

Boomers are a diverse and complex group, but most of them are hoping they will be able to control how they transition to later life. It is not surprising, then, that so many boomers plan to downsize, insisting they will not alter their lifestyles so much as compress them.

Often they want to age in the company of friends. What better way to transition into later life than with a few chosen companions? In fact, this may be just another example of the mentality of downsizing.

Boomers could someday be drawn to cohousing so that they can live in intentional communities with friends or with people who share their politics, hopes, and aspirations. In the United States today, there are already more than two hundred cohousing communities that are forming or completed. But very few of them are for people aged fifty-five and older. The time has not yet come for boomers to create cohousing of their own.

But some of them are now actively involved in something just as interesting: communities where people moved in, became friendly, and then encouraged their own friends to join them there. The following projects are wonderful examples of such unintentional community formation. Both of them are composed mostly, but not exclusively, of boomers. The original residents never planned to be living in the company of friends, but they are now doing exactly that.

SOUTH PARK LOFTS

Seattle, Washington

This is a multifamily project in a gentrifying neighborhood. Architect Chris Camarda is proud to say that these 4-Star, LEED-certified lofts are among the greenest projects his Seattle-based firm has ever done. But it took more than some prestigious certification to make South Park Lofts into the social hub that it is today.

What it took was people who have similar goals and interests. People may have moved there as strangers, but they quickly discovered that they had a lot in common, in terms of their politics and demographics. After the lofts opened in 2006, they began to attract ecominded couples and singles. Their connection to one another has deepened over the years. South Park Lofts is still known as a green community, but it is also known for its garage sales, art shows, and, according to one resident, "awesome parties."

The architectural design makes it conducive to living in the company of friends. South Park Lofts consists of four units that face each other across a commons, which runs the length of the housing unit. It did not take long for the commons to become the place where residents (and their friends) from all units would socialize.

The green/sustainable aura of the South Park district attracted like-minded boomers. Solar panels also serve as a protective awning.

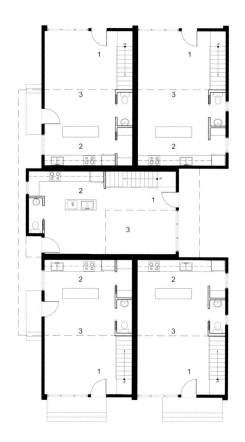

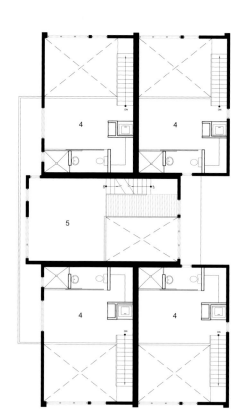

1. Entry
2. Kitchen
3. Living/Dining
4. Sleeping Loft
5. Flex Loft
6. Bedroom

Patios, common
areas, and recessed
entries give residents
opportunities to mingle
and congregate

The loft space was
particularly appealing to
childless couples and
empty nesters, who
did not have to worry
about child proofing.
Stairs and railings can
be modified in the
future, and the polished
concrete floor has
sufficient visual interest
without carpeting.

KEVIN DEFRIETAS ARCHITECTS

Row Homes on F

San Diego, California

Judging from the parties, potluck dinners, and ever-popular "Havana Nights," it would seem as if everybody living in this residential complex had been friends for years. In reality, this fun-loving "community" developed unexpectedly, thanks to the U.S. Postal Service.

Most of the people who bought the seventeen row houses in the complex are boomers and urban professionals with careers in downtown San Diego. Originally, the residents were polite but uninvolved with one another. But that changed when the postmaster refused to permit letter carriers to insert mail into the spring slots in the front doors. Because they did not meet Postal Service requirements, deFrietas was compelled to create a new freestanding block of aluminum, apartment-style mailboxes. He built them in the courtyard of the complex, and he added a bench or two. This became the spot where residents congregated and gradually formed friendships with one another.

The friendships then mellowed into a sense of community. There is now a waiting list, as friends of the residents are hoping to move in. Row Homes on F is a quintessential example of living among neighbors evolving into living among friends.

The open-loft layout, with a single bedroom, is particularly attractive to boomers who might be empty nesters, childless, or divorced.

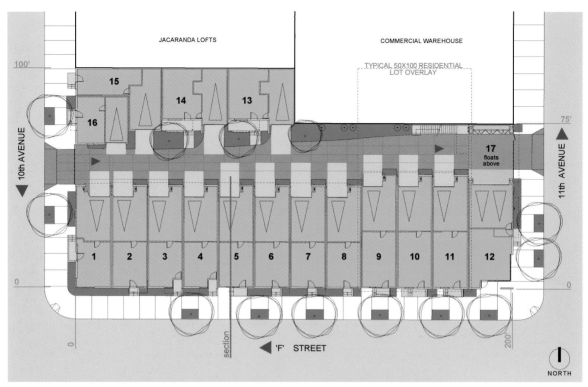

JACARANDA LOFTS

COMMERCIAL WAREHOUSE

TYPICAL 50X100 RESIDENTIAL LOT OVERLAY

100'

15

14   13

16

75'

17
floats
above

10th AVENUE

11th AVENUE

1   2   3   4   5   6   7   8   9   10   11   12

0   0

0   200'

section

'F'   STREET

NORTH

52'   35'

STOR.

PATIO   PWDR   PATIO

GARAGE

DINING   BATH

DN

KITCHEN   BEDROOM   DN

BATH

UP   UP

0

WORK
SPACE   LIVING   DECK

ENTRY

0   17'

STOOP

0   16'

01   02   03
FLOOR   FLOOR   FLOOR

The layout of the
homes is designed
to be flexible. The
lower level live-work
zone can become a
bedroom for a tenant
or caregiver.

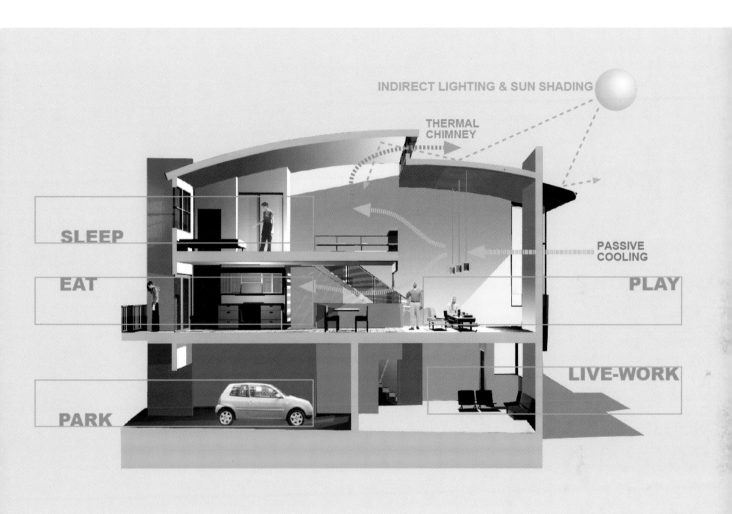

INDIRECT LIGHTING & SUN SHADING

THERMAL
CHIMNEY

SLEEP

PASSIVE
COOLING

EAT

PLAY

LIVE-WORK

PARK

Spaces open onto
one another to
maximize sociability.

AGELESS HOMES FOR LATER LIFE

Judging from their designs, the houses in this chapter are a lot like boomers themselves: they know and respect the rules, but bend them when they need to. Every one of these homes is designed for people who could someday be frail or unsteady on their feet.

Most of the residences are on one level, as if to anticipate ambulatory problems. The multilevel structures have home elevators or shaft space where elevators could someday be built. All of these homes have guest suites, or in one case a poolside cabana, which could someday be converted into living space for a caregiver. For now, though, these are only contingency plans.

In the meantime, these are spaces for gracious living, where the residents can continue finding pleasure in their careers, hobbies, fundraising, athletics, and family. The homes reflect the achievements and the whimsy of their owners.

Some of these houses are playful. One, on the beach in Venice, California, is as cool and reflective as the sunglasses worn on the boardwalk. Another has a pistachio-nut frieze, a playful reference to the couple who live there. They are successful pistachio farmers who have now moved a little closer to the city but can still manage their farm from the house.

One home is a showcase for the beautiful teakwood furniture designed by the boomer couple who live there. And a retired couple has built a beer-making room in their house.

Finally, there is the home of a married couple who value their privacy but also wanted space where they could entertain or hold small outdoor fundraisers. Like many other boomers, they decided to retrofit an existing home rather than move. They now have time and space for themselves, as well as for their charitable activities.

Someday it may be necessary for all of these homes to become more focused on healing and home care. But for now, the designs encourage the inhabitants to enjoy themselves.

BERKSHIRE RESIDENCE

Dallas, Texas

The owners of this house are a boomer couple who design teakwood furniture and own a string of showrooms where their pieces are sold. This is a second marriage for both the husband, who is in his sixties, and the wife, who is younger. Upon marrying, they decided to build their own home, which is furnished with their trademark teakwood designs.

A step-free, well-lit entry with a smooth paving surface makes the house easily accessible to all.

All living spaces and the master suite are on the ground floor. Bedrooms on the second floor are for guests or a future caregiver. The patio, designed for indoor/outdoor entertaining, has a smooth surface that is suitable for people of all ages.

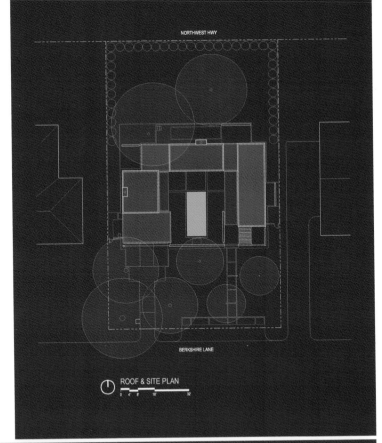

ROOF & SITE PLAN

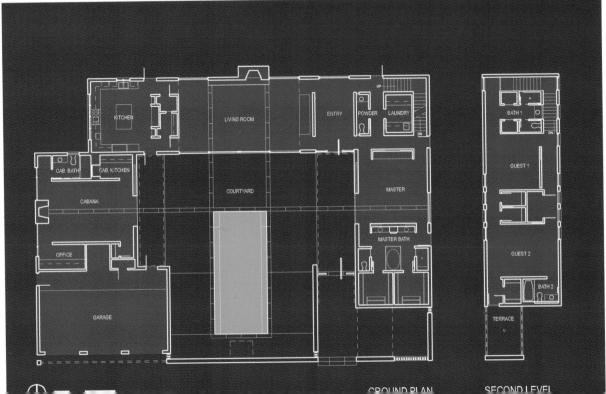

GROUND PLAN   SECOND LEVEL

The furniture, designed by the owners, has solid arms that facilitate getting up and down. There is ample space between the pieces for ease of navigation.

Panel House

Venice Beach, California

Built on the boardwalk of bustling Venice Beach, this home is able to be part of the scene in this "happening" community, but also insulated from it. This is the benefit of using sustainable materials that are highly reflective. In interesting ways, Panel House functions in the same way as sunglasses. Its reflective exterior makes the house a "mirror" where passersby can admire themselves. Those same materials create shade and absolute privacy for the people living inside.

Hertz created a house that is showy, along with having abundant ecofriendly features. Panel House is completely solar radiant heated. It has solar thermal hot water, all natural ventilation, and a potable pit. The reflective exterior is composed of prefabricated refrigerator panels clad in aluminum. The sustainable qualities of Panel House give it a small carbon footprint, but according to Hertz, they also make it perfect for the voyeurism of this beachside community.

This solar radiant heated house on the boardwalk of the Venice beach was designed for a divorced father who is the custodial parent of two teenagers.

The reflective glass minimizes glare and allows the owner to be in the most public of settings while enjoying a certain degree of privacy—an allusion to the sunglasses that beachgoers wear.

OPPOSITE Like most boomers, the owner prefers to use the stairs now, but he can rely on the glass pneumatic elevator if necessary.

ABOVE AND RIGHT Both the master bedroom suite and the living areas have expansive views of the beach.

Ross Street House

Madison, Wisconsin

Architect Carol Richard and her husband, a mechanical engineer, spent most of their professional lives in Atlanta, where Richard was the founding partner in the architecture firm Richard Wittschiebe Hand. Like many boomers, she and her husband saw their retirement as a "new beginning." In 2005 they began working on Ross Street House, where they could age in place, spend time with their grandchildren, and enjoy the Midwest, where they had both grown up. As she puts it, "We wanted the Madison lifestyle while we were still young enough to enjoy it."

The house was recognized as Wisconsin's first LEED for Homes Platinum–rated residence in July 2009. The sustainable home references the scale and building materials of houses in the surrounding neighborhood. The main level is an open plan with service elements on the west side and living spaces on the east side. The upper level contains a study opening onto the living room and master bedroom suite. The lower level has additional bedrooms, a beer-making room, and workrooms. All three levels are connected by an open stair anchored by a three-story wall.

The house is designed with shaft space for an elevator, and the cabana adjacent to the pool could be converted into a caregiver's quarters, since it includes a kitchen and bathroom.

The owners are determined to remain in this house. Of the three levels, one dedicated to grandchildren and guests is below grade. The entry level is zoned for dining and entertainment with the master suite and work spaces above.

01 FOYER
02 LIVING ROOM
03 DINING AREA
04 DEN
05 KITCHEN
06 PANTRY
07 BATHROOM
08 FUTURE ELEVATOR
09 LAUNDRY ROOM
10 SCREEN PORCH
11 DECK

01 RUMPUS ROOM
02 BEDROOM
03 BATHROOM
04 BEER MAKING ROOM
05 MECHANICAL
06 WORKROOM
07 LARDER (COLD CELLAR)
08 FUTURE ELEVATOR

A smooth path and
broad steps make the
entry easy to access.

Natural light fills the living space through sliding glass doors that connect to the terrace outside.

While the stairs to the office area and master suite might seem challenging to maneuver with age, there is a shaft connecting the three levels for a future elevator.

Zannon Building

Santa Barbara, California

Boomers do not necessarily retire when they enter their sixties. The couple who commissioned this playful home in Santa Barbara are a prime example, according to architect Jeff Shelton. He and Gail Shelton designed Zannon for a lighthearted couple with grown children, who operate a successful pistachio farm in Montecito.

The administrative work for the farm is done in Santa Barbara, and this couple decided it was time to have a place where they could live and also work. They plan to grow old here, so the architects included an elevator.

The house references the familiar architecture of Santa Barbara—white walls, red-tiled roofs, and archways—but adds playful touches that are reminiscent of Gaudí and Dalí. There are images of the pistachio nut carved into the exterior trim of the house. Four "rugs" seem to hang from a second-floor balcony, though on closer inspection, it turns out that they are not rugs at all. They are ornamental panels made of hand-painted tile that reference classic Morrish designs.

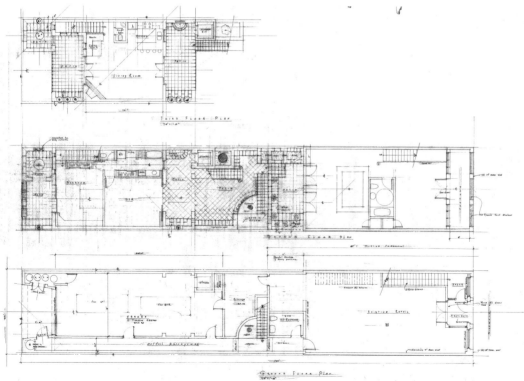

The house gives the owners proximity to downtown shops and culture, as the front suggests (above) while the rear (below) is grass-free, eliminating time-econsuming yard work and allowing easy vehicular access.

The interiors are
designed in the
mission style, with
whitewashed walls,
beamed ceilings, and
a corner fireplace.
An elevator allows
the owners to get
up and down in the
three-story house
more easily.

Stonehedge Residence

West Lake Hills, Texas

With a daughter in college, this couple needed to rethink the meaning of "home" as they moved into later life. The couple enjoyed their privacy, but they wanted to become more involved with their friends and do more fundraising for favorite charities and causes.

Like many boomers, they decided to retrofit their existing home rather than move. The couple created a great room by renovating an existing room, eliminating the second floor above to create a double-height space. The great room is anchored on one side by a nineteen-foot-tall copper-clad fireplace. On the opposite side, the room flows into a spacious terrace through a glazed wall full of large sliding doors.

To create a clear hierarchy of space in the house, the great room was expanded to a double-height volume.

ABOVE The travertine terrace links the house with the garden and pool below. An aluminum trellis, designed to accommodate two existing trees, covers the space.

OPPOSITE A monumental copper-clad pivot door welcomes guests to the house.

OVERLEAF The great room and terrace create a generous entertaining space for fund-raising events for the causes the owners support as well as for private piano recitals. Broad steps can serve as seating areas for large gatherings.

AFFORDABLE BUT NEVER BORING

The recession and sub-prime mortgage crisis have made many people in their early sixties rethink their retirement plans, which might have included ideas for a "dream house." Some are scaling back on the size and cost and choosing less expensive cost locations—assuming they even decide to relocate.

Fortunately, there is a new breed of affordable houses, town houses, and condominiums that are designed to be sustainable, welcoming, and attractive. They are a reminder that affordable housing does not have to be boring or solitary. Some of the housing has been designed to create a sense of community, while other designs aim to restore or revitalize a community. Sometimes the excitement about such housing is intentional, as in the New Orleans project known as Make It Right, NOLA, but sometimes it is refreshingly unintentional. It's attractive to boomers because it gives them a sense of "mission," a sense that they are part of the solution.

3 in a Row

San Diego, California

The houses in this row are thoughtfully designed, carefully resolved, and surprisingly affordable. The group consists of three units, all of which include a bedroom and full bathroom at ground level, as well as on-site parking. The second level contains the family room, dining room, and kitchen, with more bedrooms and baths and a balcony on level three.

Clerestory windows make these homes feel light and allow for maximum circulation of air (there is no air-conditioning at 3 in a Row). The clerestory windows also minimize the need for interior lighting during daylight hours. The exterior is mostly stucco, with very little painted surface to maintain.

Architect Kevin deFreitas says that the budget-minded boomers and forty-somethings who live here appreciate the energy efficiency and low maintenance. But most of all, they appreciate the location: many of San Diego's prime attractions are just a short walk from the front doors. Three in a Row is also near work for each of the residents.

DeFreitas predicts that the resident families will age in place. All three of the houses have space where elevators could be built if residents ever need them. "It's an affordable place to live," the architect says, "and an affordable place to grow old."

The three houses combine cost-effective materials and unornamented surfaces with a generous double-height living space.

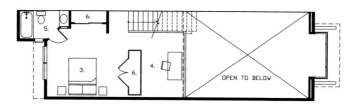

THIRD FLOOR PLAN

1. ENTRY
2. GARAGE
3. BED
4. OFFICE
5. BATH
6. CL./PNTRY
7. KITCHEN
8. DINING
9. LIVING
10. PATIO
11. YARD
12. DECK

OPEN TO BELOW

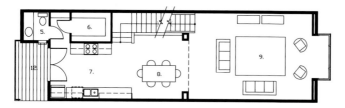

SECOND FLOOR PLAN

FIRST FLOOR PLAN

3 in a Row is part
of the renaissance
of downtown
San Diego.

The interior is zoned
for maximum flex-
ibility with the living
space on the second
floor and bedrooms
above and below.
The ground floor
bedroom can also be
used as an office.

Make It Right, NOLA

New Orleans, Louisiana

Some of the most exciting and affordable single-family homes can be found in New Orleans, rising from the wreckage of the flood-ravaged city. Brad Pitt's nonprofit Make It Right Foundation has worked with world-renowned architects to design green and affordable single-family homes for displaced residents of the Lower 9th Ward, whose homes were destroyed by Hurricane Katrina and its aftermath. Many of the homes are attracting three-generation families, often headed by people in their early sixties.

In addition to helping 150 families come home, Make It Right is helping to rebuild the community, complete with native landscaping, microfarms, rain gardens, and even new streets. Make It Right gardens are being created at the Martin Luther King school, the Village (a neighborhood center), and the Tekrema Center.

Most of the boomers living in MIR homes are not retired, or even on the verge of retirement. They are busy getting their lives and their families back on track in the aftermath of Katrina.

Tim Duggan, a spokesperson for the Make It Right development, says that as of 2011, with 80 houses already built, approximately 40 percent of homeowners living here are between the ages of 55 and 65. Each of the 1,200 square-foot homes cost $150,000 (with loans for as much as $75,000 available to displaced residents of the 9th Ward). Make It Right NOLA is giving these residents the opportunity to restore their homes and revive their community. Most important, MIR homes give peace of mind to families that were traumatized by Katrina. All of them are designed to withstand floodwaters, either because they are raised, or in the case of Float House, can actually float above flood water, should there be another Katrina.

SHIGERU BAN ARCHITECTS

This three-bedroom home on Tennessee Street, known as Furniture House 6, is occupied by a retired college professor. The design reinvents traditional nineteenth-century shotgun house, including a front porch and sharply pitched roof. It is built of low-cost, pre-fabricated elements that create a series of flexible rooms. The house offers a shady porch where family and friends can congregate and watch the world go by. The front door opens onto a large, square living room with a kitchen in one corner, and a small island counter separating the two spaces. Stilts raise the building above ground level to help withstand flooding.

The rigorous, post-Katrina building code mandates that houses be raised a minimum of five feet above the ground.

OPPOSITE ABOVE A wall of cubes provides stylish storage and eliminates the need for handles and drawers.

OPPOSITE BELOW An external stair descends to the patio.

ABOVE Solar panels on the gabled roof and a green roof on the bedroom wing contributed to the LEED Platinum rating for the house.

PUGH + SCARPA   This is home to a married couple and their two
teenaged children. Instead of shotgun-style rooms
all in a row, Pugh + Scarpa gave this family a set of
multi-purpose "zones" that can be used for entertaining, sleepovers, or a home office. An important
goal was to create a home that would continue to
be relevant as family members grow up and needs
change.

The house is built of recycled wooden pallets,
making it both green and sustainable. The design
builds visually upon traditional American patchwork motifs as well as the early Southern rural
tradition of insulating walls with newspapers and
magazines. But it incorporates current technologies
to keep it affordable and better able to withstand
the forces of nature.

Inspired by American
patchwork quilting
traditions, the
exterior is wrapped
in a shade screen
composed of
recycled wooden
pallets joined by
perforated cement
board,

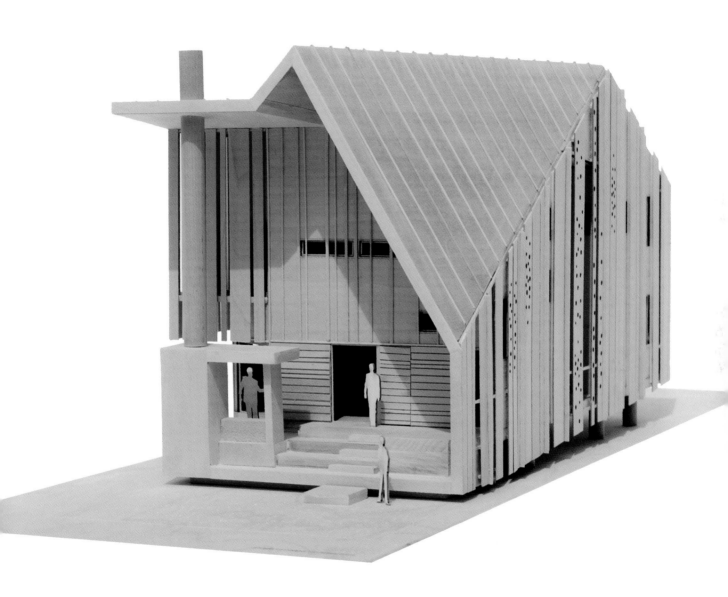

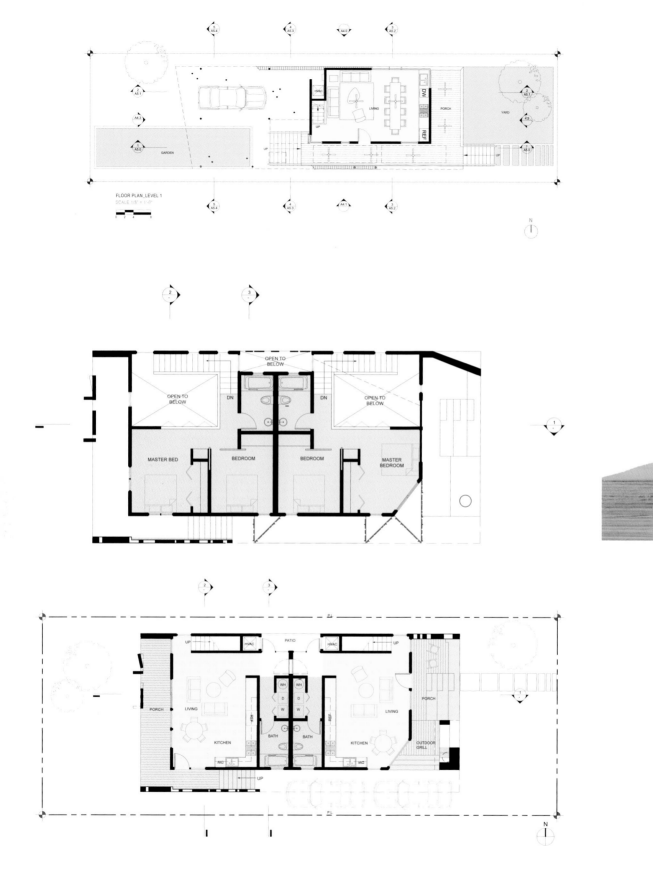

FLOOR PLAN_LEVEL 1
SCALE 1/8" = 1'-0"

The house is designed
with flexible zones
rather than distinct
rooms so the layout
can be changed as
the occupant ages in
place and household
composition changes.

ADJAYE ASSOCIATES

Katrina destroyed more than buildings in the 9th Ward. It also obliterated the lively and sociable front-porch culture. To restore that pleasure, Adjaye added a grand staircase to the side of the house facing Deslande Street. That staircase has become a place for friends and neighbors to sit and socialize, for grandchildren to play, and for grandparents to watch the world go by. An open patio on the roof offers panoramic views of New Orleans and could be "high ground" if necessary. This is a home that provides both connection and peace of mind.

The gutter surrounding the open light shaft collects rainwater to be used for irrigation and cleaning.

ABOVE An upper terrace allows for shelter from the sun but is also a high-ground place of refuge in the event of a major flood. Bleacher-scale steps running next to the entry stairs allow people to gather on the front stoop. The bottom step acts as a bench along the sidewalk.

MORPHOSIS ARCHITECTS   Home to a retired couple, this design re-imagines the traditional shotgun house in a new, flood-proof incarnation. In the event of another Katrina, the entire house could rise twelve feet on the four posts that anchor it to the ground. For all of its technology, Float House is still affordable. And it is very much in the social tradition of the 9th Ward. Float House has reinvented the front porch with an entry that allows family and friends to gather while being designed for accessibility so that elderly and disabled friends feel just as welcome.

A green ramp makes the house accessible to all.

FLOAT HOUSE: PARTS

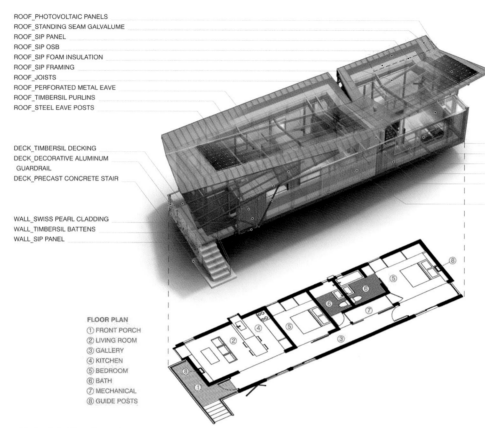

ROOF_PHOTOVOLTAIC PANELS
ROOF_STANDING SEAM GALVALUME
ROOF_SIP PANEL
ROOF_SIP OSB
ROOF_SIP FOAM INSULATION
ROOF_SIP FRAMING
ROOF_JOISTS
ROOF_PERFORATED METAL EAVE
ROOF_TIMBERSIL PURLINS
ROOF_STEEL EAVE POSTS

GALLERY_POLYCARBONATE
CLERESTORY ROOF
RAINWATER COLLECTION TANKS
GALLERY_WINDOW FRAMING
GALLERY_ STEEL DECK SUPPORTS
PHOTOVOLTAIC BATTERY STORAGE
GALLERY_POLYCARBONATE
HURRICANE SHUTTER

DECK_TIMBERSIL DECKING
DECK_DECORATIVE ALUMINUM
GUARDRAIL
DECK_PRECAST CONCRETE STAIR

WALL_SWISS PEARL CLADDING
WALL_TIMBERSIL BATTENS
WALL_SIP PANEL

FLOOR PLAN
① FRONT PORCH
② LIVING ROOM
③ GALLERY
④ KITCHEN
⑤ BEDROOM
⑥ BATH
⑦ MECHANICAL
⑧ GUIDE POSTS

Kitchen work surfaces are designed to be open and accessible. The contrast of white and black surfaces makes it easier for aging eyes to make distinctions.

PHOTOGRAPHY CREDITS

Numbers refer to page numbers.

Alise O'Brien Photography: 155, 156 bottom

Arakawa + Gins: 147

Dustin Askland: 158 bottom, 162, 163 top and bottom left

Farshid Assassi/Assassi Production: 19, 21, 22, 23

Iwan Baan: 234, 236, 237

Barrett Studio Architects: 119 top, 123 top left

CJ Chapman: 49

Bo Crockett: 81, 82–83, 85, 86, 87

David Hewitt & Anne Garrison Architectural Photography: 215, 217, 218, 219

David Fenton: 52 bottom

Paul Finkel/Piston Design: 207, 208, 209, 210–11

Tim Griffith: 63, 64, 65

Anice Hoachlander: 68, 69, 71, 72, 73

Jerry Butts Photography: 150, 152–53, 156 top, 157

John Linden: 38, 41, 42, 43, 44, 45

Rafael Longoria: 223, 224, 225

Maxwell MacKenzie: 124, 127, 129 top

Björg Magnea: 24, 27, 28, 29, 30, 31

Wayne McCall: 201, 202, 203, 204, 205

Scott McGlashan: 51, 52 top, 54, 55

Miró Rivera Architects: 78–79

Jurgen Nogai: 186, 188, 189, 190, 191

Chris Pardo: 109, 110, 112, 113

Carol Peerce: 172, 176, 177

Paul Bardagjy Photography: 96, 99, 100, 101, 139, 140, 141, 142, 143

Paul Warchol Photography: 126, 129 bottom, 130, 131

Jose Luis Perez-Griffo Viquera: 145 top

Joke Post: 149

Paul Richer: 103, 104, 107

Najela Shamah: 167, 169, 170, 171

Shimer © Hedrich Blessing: 91, 93, 94, 95

Charles Smith: 33, 35, 36, 37, 181, 183, 184, 185

Sparano + Mooney Architecture: 106, 158 top, 160, 161, 163 bottom right

Brian Vanden Brink: 117, 118, 119 bottom, 120, 121, 122, 123 top right and bottom

James Weil: 133, 134, 135 ,136, 137

Jim Westphalen: 56, 59, 60, 61

Zane Williams: 193, 195, 196, 197, 198, 199

Patrick Wong/Atelier Wong Photography: 75, 76, 77

Dimitris Yeros: 145 bottom, 148